ELIZABETH REVEALED

500 facts about The Queen and her world

Lucinda Hawksley

Historic
Royal Palaces

CONTENTS

Foreword

There is a certain irony in the fact that in this age of mass communication we have far fewer of Her Majesty Queen Elizabeth II's remarks, speeches and opinions on record than those of her predecessors. For example, Queen Victoria's voluminous diaries provide a vivid sense of her character, thoughts and beliefs. We know what her feelings were when she first set eyes upon Prince Albert, the depths of her despair when he died, and the disappointment and frustration that motherhood often brought to her. Likewise, the official state papers and private correspondence of monarchs as wide-ranging as Edward III, Mary I and George IV make them knowable in a way that our current queen never has been.

What we do know about Elizabeth II is her unwavering sense of duty and the constant, stabilising presence she has given to the monarchy during the course of her long reign. Those qualities might not grab history headlines in the same way as Henry VIII, the king who married six times, his daughter Elizabeth, the Virgin Queen, or perhaps George III, the so-called 'mad' king. But the very lack of drama has been the secret of The Queen's success.

That is not to say that Elizabeth II's reign has been unremarkable: far from it. It has witnessed an almost unimaginable scale of change, from a revolution in technology and communications to the transformation of Britain into a diverse and multicultural society. Along the way, The Queen herself has broken all sorts of records – longest reigning monarch in the world, highest number of countries visited by a British sovereign, longest marriage in British royal history, to name but a few. She has also introduced new legislation giving equal pre-eminence to female heirs in the succession – a subtle but revolutionary change.

Historic Royal Palaces has enjoyed a long association with Queen Elizabeth II. We manage six extraordinary palaces on her behalf, and she has remained closely engaged with each of them during the course of her long reign. The crown jewels with which she was adorned at her coronation in June 1953 are housed in the Tower of London and admired by millions of visitors every year. In 1956 The Queen visited the London Museum at Kensington Palace, following the reopening of the State Apartments. She has since loaned numerous dresses for display at the palace, most recently for the hugely popular *Fashion Rules* exhibition in 2013 and its sequel in 2016. The following year it was the turn of Hampton Court to welcome both The Queen and the Duke of Edinburgh to a special evensong service in the Chapel Royal, which was held to commemorate the centenary of the Order of the Companions of Honour. Since April 2014 Historic Royal Palaces has also been responsible for Hillsborough Castle, The Queen's official residence in Northern Ireland. Her Majesty has stayed here regularly during her reign, notably as part of her Silver Jubilee tour in 1977.

These are just some of the myriad connections that the palaces in our care have enjoyed with Elizabeth II. A few of them feature in the fascinating selection of facts that follow, all 500 of which reveal a surprising new aspect of Her Majesty The Queen. Taken together, they challenge the assumption that she is somehow unknowable. By the end of it, I felt I had become much better acquainted with this most private of queens.

Tracy Borman
Joint Chief Curator, Historic Royal Palaces

4

Princess Elizabeth in 1936, in the garden of her London home at 145 Piccadilly.

Introduction

In 2002, the year of her Golden Jubilee, Queen Elizabeth II addressed Parliament with a speech that included the words, 'Change is a constant; managing it has become an expanding discipline. The way we embrace it defines our future.' Those sentences are emblematic of her reign.

When Princess Elizabeth came to the throne in 1952, few could have foreseen the tremendous changes that would take place during her decades as queen. She has beaten her great-great-grandmother, Queen Victoria, to become the longest-serving monarch in British history, she has witnessed the arrival and departure of other monarchies, world leaders, dictatorships and political regimes, throughout all of which she has remained at the helm, as queen not only of Great Britain and Ireland, but of the Commonwealth. Following the death of King Bhumibol Adulyadej of Thailand in 2016, Queen Elizabeth II became the world's longest-reigning monarch. Her image can be seen on currencies and postage stamps throughout the world, she has been photographed incessantly, and painted and sculpted at every moment of her reign. Her image has become internationally iconic.

The Queen has presided over an era of wide-ranging, and often mesmerising, changes. In 1952 only 14 per cent of households in Britain owned a television set, yet by the time of her much-celebrated 90th birthday in 2016, 95 per cent of people in Britain owned a mobile phone – using technology that hadn't even been thought of when she became queen. She has watched the tentative beginnings of the National Health Service grow into one of the country's most important employers, providing medical services that would have seemed miraculous in the 1950s: organ transplants, IVF babies, effective cancer treatments and cures for illnesses that hadn't even been heard of at the start of her reign.

As the new Elizabethan era dawned, Britain was still struggling to recover from the Second World War. The nation was grieving for its dead, people were trying to build a new, post-war world on a very limited national budget, and food rationing was still in force. When Elizabeth became queen, tea, sugar, butter, cheese, cooking fat and meat were still being rationed; today the variety and choice of foods in British shops and markets is almost overwhelming. In 21st-century Britain, people think nothing of eating food hailing from all over the globe, with many Chinese, Italian and Indian dishes now thought of as 'traditional' British fare. In the 1950s, however, there were very few foreign cuisines on offer, popular foods such as spaghetti, hummus or avocados were almost unheard of in the UK, and olive oil was sold in chemist shops as a medicinal aid – only the brave few would have thought of eating it! Today no self-respecting British kitchen can be imagined without an array of exotic cooking oils and cookery books boasting recipes from every corner of the world map. The UK's multicultural population has also helped to create a vibrant change in the worlds of British music, fashion and culture.

At the beginning of her reign, The Queen had been married for just five years and was a young mother; today she is a great-grandmother, and she and the Duke of Edinburgh have been married for over seven decades. Throughout their marriage, The Queen and her husband have visited over 120 countries, and driven in every type of vehicle imaginable. They have flown over mountains, sailed over oceans, journeyed by trains on exotic tracks, ridden horses on several continents, travelled by supersonic plane and golden carriage, and been entertained by world leaders of all political styles, while unfamiliar wildlife has prowled the grounds around them and crowds have lined the streets for miles to catch a glimpse of the most famous woman in the world.

The Queen has seen 13 Prime Ministers come and go, and has welcomed hundreds of heads of state to Britain. She has seen extraordinary societal change, lived through wars and terrorism, learnt about incredible medical and technological breakthroughs, been challenged by previously unthinkable personal attacks in the media, and watched as the legal, political and criminal justice systems have undergone rigorous changes. Queen Elizabeth II has led her Royal Family from the days when it was expected to be closed off and unapproachable, discouraged from revealing any emotion, through a sea change of monumental proportions. She has spearheaded her family's changing role in dealing with the public and the media, and she has encouraged a welcome openness in the younger generations of royals.

Whilst helping to bring about this much-needed change to a more approachable monarchy, The Queen has been able to retain her extremely private self. Perhaps she has enjoyed being able to remain something of an enigma – to the extent that even her own family had no idea she had agreed to play a starring role in the 2012 Olympics Opening Ceremony, until the performance itself!

The image of Queen Elizabeth II is not only instantly recognisable in her own country and around the Commonwealth, but all over the globe. She appears again and again in lists of the world's most powerful people and her image appears regularly in newspapers worldwide. She grew up in the spotlight and had to create the role of a 21st-century monarch through years of hard-fought and dedicated training, with limited guidance about what being a monarch in the modern age would entail. The Queen was just 25 years old when her father's death projected her onto the world stage; in 2017 she celebrated 65 years on the throne. Throughout those decades, she has been forced to perform as monarch, to raise her family, to work on her marriage, to learn from her mistakes and to confront her sadnesses, whilst all the time being the focus of the world's cameras.

Since the time of her much-scrutinised wedding and coronation, The Queen has changed – and the public, the role of the monarchy, her country and the Commonwealth have changed almost beyond recognition, yet she has continued to work effectively and tirelessly, even after celebrating her 90th birthday. To many observers Queen Elizabeth II is the epitome of a regal monarch, but to her great-grandbabies, she is simply the much-adored 'Gan Gan'.

ELIZABETH AS A GIRL

The abdication of her uncle, in 1936, transformed young Princess Elizabeth's life forever. Her shy father, the Duke of York, succeeded to the throne as George VI and Elizabeth, unexpectedly, became his heir. However, until she was 10, happily oblivious to the immensity of her future role, Elizabeth enjoyed the life of a minor royal. Doted on by her parents, the 'little darling with a lovely complexion' was brought up, as were other aristocratic children, by nurses and nannies, and her beloved governess, 'Crawfie'. A keen swimmer and rider, Elizabeth had dogs, ponies, and even her own private Girl Guide unit, the 1st Buckingham Palace Girl Guide Company.

A 15-month-old Princess Elizabeth, seated on one of her first 'thrones'.

Birth and childhood

Three tonnes of baby presents, a governess, and her own Girl Guide pack… little about Princess Elizabeth's early years can be described as 'ordinary'. Yet she was born into a loving family, expected to be a fairly minor royal, until her life was changed forever aged 10, when her uncle abdicated.

1 Princess Elizabeth Alexandra Mary, known in her family as 'Lilibet', was named after her mother, her grandmother and her great-grandmother. She was born on 21 April 1926, by caesarean section. Her grandmother, Queen Mary, recorded in her diary that the new baby was 'a little darling with a lovely complexion and fair hair'.

2 The Princess was born at her parents' home, 17 Bruton Street, in London's expensive and fashionable Mayfair. The house was owned by her mother's family, the Bowes-Lyons. Unfortunately, the house no longer survives.

3 It was revealed to the public that the baby's layette included clothes handmade by her grandmothers, Queen Mary and Lady Strathmore, and her mother, the Duchess of York.

4 Because her father had an older brother, Princess Elizabeth was third in line to the throne, but as a girl, it seemed unlikely that she would ever be monarch. It was expected that her uncle would marry and have children who would be ahead of her. It also seemed likely that she would have younger brothers, all of whom would automatically take precedence over her.

5 When the Princess was 9 months old, her parents embarked on a six-month tour, leaving her in the care of her nurse 'Allah' and her grandparents, the King and Queen. Her parents travelled by ocean liner to Latin America, through the Panama Canal, then on to Fiji, New Zealand and Australia. At every stop, the Duke and Duchess were given baby presents – one estimate suggested the presents alone weighed three tonnes.

Opposite page: **(top) Princess Elizabeth on wheels, 1930. (Bottom left) A hand tinted postcard of Princesses Elizabeth and Margaret with their mother in 1936. (Bottom right) Elizabeth, fourth from left, at a birthday party in 1935.**

This page: **(left) Princesses in panto – Elizabeth and Margaret perform 'Aladdin and the Princess' at Windsor Castle in 1943. (Below) Princess Elizabeth riding in Windsor Great Park, 1934.**

6 Elizabeth did not go away to school. She was educated at home, where one of her tutors was Henry Marten, the vice-provost of Eton (the school that her grandsons William and Harry would later attend). Marten tutored the future queen in Constitutional History.

7 As the Princess was not permitted to join a public Girl Guides' unit, her governess, Crawfie, set up a troop of carefully chosen friends, the 1st Buckingham Palace Girl Guide Company, presided over by a Miss Violet Synge. Elizabeth, then 11, begged for her younger sister Margaret Rose to be allowed to join, telling Miss Synge that Margaret had a 'fine pair of hiking legs',

adding 'she loves getting dirty'. At 7, Margaret was too young to be a Guide, so the pack was extended to include Brownies.

8 In 1940 Buckingham Palace was hit by a German bomb. A few weeks later, Princesses Elizabeth and Margaret Rose (who had been safely moved to Windsor at the time of the bomb) made a recording at the palace for the BBC's *Children's Hour.* Elizabeth read out a short speech, which included the lines: 'I want you all to be very good and to do just as you're told and take great care of your gas masks. I've got one, too, I've been trying it on and I looked so funny in it that Rose laughed and laughed until she nearly cried!'

9 As the war progressed, the Princesses were evacuated from London, and travelled between royal residences in the countryside, including Windsor Castle, Balmoral and Sandringham. While they were at Windsor, the girls put on fund-raising pantomimes to buy material for military uniforms, through The Queen's Wool Fund.

10 In 1943 Princess Elizabeth became a Sea Ranger. The 16-year-old princess was photographed in her new uniform by Dorothy Wilding. She joined the ship SRS *President III* (later renamed the *Duke of York* by her father). After two years, Elizabeth was made Commodore of the Sea Ranger Section.

11

The Duke and Duchess of York

Princess Elizabeth's parents were a love match, her mother deeply supportive and devoted to the shy, socially awkward Duke of York. Both she and her husband put their daughters' happiness first, little thinking that they would have to step up to be King and Queen themselves, and their first born become heir to the throne.

11 The Queen's father was born at York Cottage, Sandringham, on 14 December 1895. As a child he was known as Prince Albert, and in 1920 he was given the titles of Baron Killarney, Earl of Inverness, and Duke of York. He was known in the family as 'Bertie', but when he acceded to the throne, he chose to be crowned King George VI.

12 The Queen's mother was born Lady Elizabeth Angela Marguerite Bowes-Lyon, on 4 August 1900. She was the youngest daughter of the 14th Earl and Countess of Strathmore. Lady Elizabeth had three sisters and six brothers, one of whom was killed in action during the First World War.

13 The Duke of York served in both the Royal Navy and the Royal Air Force. In 1916 he was present at the Battle of Jutland on board *The Iron Duke*, the flagship of Admiral Jellicoe's fleet. Towards the end of the war he was attached to the Headquarters Staff of the RAF, which helped organise the air-raid reprisals against Germany.

F.A. SWAINE.

TH
RO
WEL

ALL HAPPINESS

Left: A young Prince Albert, or 'Bertie' to his family, photographed in fashionable sailor suit in 1904.
Main image: A souvenir postcard celebrating the royal wedding of the Duke of York to Elizabeth Bowes-Lyon on 26 April 1923.

Below: The Duke of York on board HMS *Collingswood* in 1915, and enjoying a relaxing ride at the Great Bookham fete, 1922.

L
NG

F. A. SWAINE.

ATTEND THEM.

The coronation of her parents was Princess Elizabeth's first major royal occasion. She and Princess Margaret wore lightweight coronets of silver gilt. (Below) The Queen Mother during her 101st birthday celebrations.

14 The Duke proposed to Lady Elizabeth Bowes-Lyon three times, the first time in 1921. She turned him down twice because she was, 'afraid never, never again to be free to think, speak and act as I feel I really ought to'. She finally accepted him in January 1923 and they were married on 26 April 1923, in Westminster Abbey.

15 The Duchess of York was the last royal mother required to give birth in the presence of the Home Secretary, who was there (in an adjoining room!) to ensure that the royal baby was not swapped for a smuggled-in 'imposter'. The birth of Princess Elizabeth was attended by Sir William Joynson-Hicks, and that of Princess Margaret by John Robert ('JR') Clynes. This practice ended in 1948, shortly before Prince Charles was born.

16 The coronation of her parents on 12 May 1937 was the first major royal occasion that Princess Elizabeth attended. Elizabeth and Margaret wore coronets made of silver gilt, as their specially commissioned gold coronets turned out to be far too heavy for the young girls to wear.

17 The Princess described their coronation in her diary, writing that Westminster Abbey was 'a sort of haze of wonder as papa was crowned, at least I thought so'. However, she also added that 'at the end of the service it got rather boring as it was all prayers. Grannie and I were looking to see how many more pages to the end...'.

18 The morale-boosting radio broadcast that George VI gave on the day war was declared with Germany was also a personal triumph. The King, who was afflicted with a stammer and speech impediment, delivered this crucial public message with great clarity, after working with the unconventional Australian speech therapist Lionel Logue. Logue continued to help the King with public speaking challenges for the rest of his life.

19 The King, mindful of how desperately unprepared he had felt when he became monarch, was determined to help his elder daughter. He may well have realised that his own poor health meant that Elizabeth would have to assume power at a young age, so he instigated 'rigorous training in public affairs and duties of a monarch' for the young Princess.

20 Queen Elizabeth The Queen Mother lived until the age of 101. She continued to carry out public duties until a few months before her death in March 2002, including being photographed on her 101st birthday in 2001 with her family at the gates of Clarence House.

Y Bwthyn Bach.

The Royal Family relaxing at Y Bwthyn
Bach (The Little Cottage) – a miniature
house in the grounds of Windsor Great
Park , given as a birthday gift to Princess
Elizabeth by the people of Wales in 1932.

Ten notable relatives and friends

Like any family, royal or otherwise, some members are closer than others. The Queen had her favourites when growing up, and she has cherished the support and loyalty of some lifelong close friends.

21 The Queen was very close to her grandfather, George V, who – despite his reputation for being bad-tempered – doted upon his granddaughter. She called him 'Grandpa England'. One day when the Archbishop of Canterbury visited the King, he found his monarch crawling on the floor on all fours, pretending to be a horse, while Princess Elizabeth led him around by his beard.

22 The Queen's younger sister, Princess Margaret Rose, was born on 21 August 1930 at Glamis Castle in Scotland, when Princess Elizabeth was 4. The Home Secretary JR Clynes, who was present at the birth, wrote of the baby, 'I am glad to say that she has large blue eyes and a will of iron, which is all the equipment a lady needs'.

23 Until Elizabeth was ten, her uncle David was a dashing but distant figure in her life, who had nicknamed her 'Shirley Temple', because of her curly hair. On the death of George V in January 1936 he was due to be crowned as Edward VIII. His passionate relationship with the

soon-to-be thrice divorced American Wallis Simpson caused deep concerns; as divorcée, she could not be crowned queen. By December that year he decided to abdicate, a decision that changed Elizabeth's destiny. Her father and mother were crowned King and Queen in 1937, and the Princess became heir to the throne.

24 On 9 September 2015 Queen Elizabeth II beat the record of 63 years and 216 days set by her great-great-grandmother, Queen Victoria (right, in 1893), and became the longest-ruling monarch in British history.

Left: **Magazine cover of 1937, celebrating the 'pin-up' princesses.** *Below left:* **Princess Elizabeth with her grandparents, George V and Queen Mary in June 1934.** *Below right:* **The Queen's uncle, Edward VIII in 1936, during his brief reign.**

Above: **Princesses Elizabeth and Margaret with their cousin and childhood friend Margaret Elphinstone in 1949.**
Below: **The Duke of Kent, with the Duchess and their two elder children Edward and Alexandra.**

25 The Queen had a remarkable great-great-aunt, *Princess Louise* (above), daughter of Queen Victoria. The unconventional Louise, whom The Queen remembered meeting, was a professional sculptor and artist who designed the statue of her mother that stands outside Kensington Palace. Louise, who died in 1939, aged 91 was the first royal to be cremated. The Queen attended her funeral at St George's Chapel, Windsor.

26 *Prince George, Duke of Kent,* was The Queen's uncle, and served in the RAF. The Royal Family was devastated when he was killed in action in 1942. The Queen has always remained close to his children, her cousins, Prince Edward, Princess Alexandra and Prince Michael (who was only weeks old when his father died).

27 *Princess Alexandra* (née of Kent) is The Queen's cousin and childhood friend. She was also a bridesmaid at The Queen's wedding. In her teens, she was known around the world for being the

first princess to have what a Canadian magazine described as 'a democratic education'. One of her schoolfriend's mothers once commented, 'Sometimes I find it difficult to remember you are a princess', to which Alexandra is reported to have replied, 'Sometimes I find it rather hard myself.'

28 *Lady Pamela Hicks* (née Mountbatten) is related by blood both to Prince Philip (who is her first cousin) and The Queen (they are third cousins). She was a bridesmaid at their wedding and, when interviewed in 2017, remembered having to 'rush' back from India (where her father was Viceroy) for the wedding, and missing most of the rehearsals.

29 *Margaret Rhodes* (née Elphinstone) was one of The Queen's cousins and childhood playmates. They were born just ten months apart. When Margaret wrote her autobiography (which she sent to The Queen for approval), she included tales of their 'blissfully happy times up in Scotland', riding ponies and going on picnics.

30 *Patrick Plunket,* 7th Baron Plunket, was a childhood friend of The Queen and became her much-trusted equerry and later the Deputy Master of the Royal Household. He was by Princess Elizabeth's side as she embarked on her journey to become Elizabeth II, while coping with her grief at her father's death.

Royal bridesmaids (left to right): Lady Pamela
Mountbatten, Princess Alexandra of Kent,
Princess Margaret and Princess Elizabeth outside
Romney Abbey in Kent in October 1946, after the
wedding of Pamela's sister Patricia to John Ullick
Knatchbull, 7th Baron Brabourne.

Ten queen makers

There have been many significant figures – some grand and powerful, some at a more intimate level – in The Queen's life. Some became very close friends, or played a key role in her life from an early age.

31 Clara Knight, known as 'Allah', was The Queen's childhood nurse, who, 25 years earlier, had nursed her mother, too! While on their Commonwealth tour in 1927, the Duke and Duchess of York received a letter 'from' their baby: 'If Mummy looks into my wide open mouth with a little magnifying glass she will see my two teeth. Elizabeth quite well and happy! Allah'.

32 Margaret Macdonald, known as 'Bobo', was The Queen's nanny, dresser and friend. She began her career with the family as under-nurse in the Duke and Duchess of York's household, under Clara Knight.

33 Both Princesses Elizabeth and Margaret adored their Scottish governess, Marion Crawford, whom they nicknamed 'Crawfie'. She had trained as a teacher and studied child psychology, and so impressed the Duke and Duchess of York that they snapped her up for their daughters. In 1950 she published a biographical book entitled *The Little Princesses*, after which she became estranged from the Royal Family.

34 The Queen is very close to her sister's daughter, Lady Sarah Chatto (née Armstrong-Jones), who is her only niece, and they enjoy spending time together. Their joint favourite hideaway is said to be Craigowan Lodge in Aberdeenshire. Lady Sarah was chief bridesmaid at the wedding of Prince Charles and Lady Diana Spencer.

35 Australian-born William Heseltine was The Queen's Press Secretary in the 1960s, and helped to modernise the Royal Family's relationship with the media. He encouraged The Queen to allow her family be filmed for a television documentary, because he felt the royals needed to be more accessible to a modern public audience. In 2015, when asked to describe The Queen for an Australian newspaper, he responded 'Elizabeth the Steadfast, or Elizabeth the Unflappable'.

36 Sir Winston Churchill was The Queen's very first Prime Minister, from 1951 to 1955, and he became a valued friend. Their weekly meetings usually lasted much longer than scheduled, but when a curious interviewer once asked him what they talked about, Churchill replied, 'Oh, mostly racing'.

37 Jean Woodroffe became Lady-in-Waiting to Princess Elizabeth in 1945. She was 22 years old and already a war widow. She was with The Queen, Princess Margaret and Margaret Rhodes when they decided to join the crowds in London on VE Day.

This page: **(left) The Queen is greeted by retiring Prime Minister Sir Winston Churchill and Lady Churchill, April 1955. (Below left) The Queen's ever-helpful Lady-in-Waiting Susan Hussey. (Below) The Queen's personal dresser, Angela Kelly.**

38 Lady Susan Hussey is The Queen's Lady-in-Waiting, and so trusted that The Queen asked her to guide the young Princess Diana, after her wedding, to help her adjust to life in the Royal Family. She is also godmother to Prince William.

39 Ann Fortune Fitzroy, the Duchess of Grafton, was named The Queen's Lady of the Bedchamber in 1953 and was later made Mistress of the Robes. She is one of The Queen's Ladies-in-Waiting. The Queen is godmother to Ann's daughter, Lady Virginia Fitzroy.

40 The Queen is renowned throughout the world for her elegant dress sense, and this is in no small part due to the work of her personal dresser, Angela Kelly. Ms Kelly was born in 1952 – the year in which Princess Elizabeth became queen – and began her illustrious career by making dresses for her dolls. She met The Queen in 1992, having previously become friendly with the Queen Mother's dresser.

ELIZABETH AS A GIRL

ELIZABETH THE WOMAN

As a young, glamorous princess, Elizabeth captured the imagination of the public, and her changing style and fashions as the years go by continue to fascinate us. Even in her nineties, her outfits and hats still attract comment in the international media. The most private of queens, Elizabeth has, over her long reign, learnt to maintain sphinx-like composure in front of the world's cameras – but informal images captured when she is with her family, or around her beloved racehorses, seem to reveal more of her personality and humour. She is an accomplished camerawoman herself; The Queen has enjoyed filming and taking photographs of her growing family and life on royal tours, when she has often been *behind* the camera.

This iconic picture of The Queen in a strapless Norman Hartnell dress was taken by Dorothy Wilding in 1952. Copies of the image were circulated to embassies around the world and appeared on stamps and bank notes.

Ten top hats

The Queen has favoured many an eye-catching hat over the years, the only rule being that it should never obscure her face. Her favourite designers have used a variety of millinery tricks to make her headgear stand out as uniquely British.

41 This unusual beret style with oversized feather was appropriately jaunty for the 1962 Braemar Highland Gathering in Scotland.

42 Described in the press as 'Sprightly feathers with a balancing bow', this hat was worn for a visit to Crawley, Sussex, in January 1950.

45 This striking red hat is a nod to Sixties style. It appeared on a royal visit to Ventnor on the Isle of Wight in 1965.

43 This bright turban would have made The Queen stand out in the sunshine of Fiji during a royal visit in 1977.

44 A lovely rose in Pacific blue for a trip to Tuvalu as part of The Queen's tour in October 1982.

46 While in Malta in 1967, The Queen chose this flowered hat to match the soft pinks and green of her outfit.

47 The Queen wore this hat with blue flowers and yellow stamens to the State Opening of Parliament on 21 June 2017, the first time in 43 years that she hadn't worn the Imperial State Crown (see also page 64). She was delivering a speech outlining Brexit plans, which prompted comment in the media that her hat bore an uncanny resemblance to the European flag. Her Majesty is, of course, politically neutral.

48 This glowing crimson hat was the perfect choice for a tour of the new Baglan Power Station in Port Talbot, South Wales, in October 2004.

49 Looking both warm and elegant, The Queen wore this hat during a walkabout in the Slovakian villa of Spisska in October 2008.

50 The Queen, resplendent in royal purple, greets well-wishers outside St Peter and St Paul's Church after Sunday service in West Newton, Norfolk, in February 2011.

Ten royal outfits

'Always age-appropriate, [The Queen's] peep-toed sandals and nipped in waists of the New Look era gave way to sleeveless shift dresses and finally more covered fashions in bright colours', wrote an admiring American journalist in *Town & Country* magazine.

51 The Queen in America in May 2007, during a visit to the Capitol Building in Virginia to commemorate the 400th anniversary of the founding of Jamestown.

52 Princess Elizabeth as a bridesmaid at the wedding of Lady May and Captain Henry Abel Smith, October 1931.

53 A snazzy leopardskin coat and ankle boots keep Her Majesty warm at Sandown racecourse on a very cold March day in 1962.

59 The Queen during a visit to the Sikh Temple in Hounslow, west London, in 2014.

54 Princess Elizabeth after a private visit to see the London Stock Exchange in action, in May 1949.

55 A glamorous Gold Cup day at Royal Ascot in 1954.

56 The Queen wore this slim fitting white lace dress, with black tulle hat, to a garden party in Sydney, Australia, in 1954.

HARDYAMIES

57 A navy and white outfit, with butcher boy cap, for a visit to a naval dockyard in San Diego in 1983.

58 A sketch by one of the Queen's favourite designers, Hardy Amies, who created her daywear for many years.

60 This elegant ensemble, worn in Ireland in 2011 was created by Stewart Parvin. He also designed the eyecatching lime green outfit worn by The Queen for the royal wedding in 2018.

61 Enjoying the craik at the English market in Cork during The Queen's 2011 visit to the Ireland. It was the first state visit to the Republic by a British monarch for a hundred years.

62 Sharing expertise: The Queen chats with an official at the Royal Windsor Horse show in May 2014.

63 A family moment after Princess Charlotte of Cambridge's christening on 5 July 2015, outside the church of St Mary Magdalene on the Sandringham Estate, Norfolk.

64 HMY *Britannia* was one of The Queen's favourite retreats, where she could escape some of the royal pressures and relax, as here in March 1972.

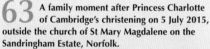

65 Celebrating success at Newbury Races in April 2013, as The Queen's horse Signal Manual wins the Drewett Handicap Stakes. Celebrating with Her Majesty are her bloodstock and racing advisor John Warren (behind) and racing trainer Michael Bell.

Royal *and* relaxed

'The Queen has a lovely laugh. She laughs with her whole face.'
Labour MP Richard Crossman

66 The Queen presents her victorious husband with the Windsor Cup after his polo team beat India during Ascot week in 1955.

67 A delighted Queen applauds as Prince Philip tackles the obstacle course for coaches at the Royal Windsor Horse show in May 1985.

68 Absorbed in the moment, The Queen watches her husband compete at the Royal Windsor Horse Show in 1982.

69 The Queen and Prince Charles enjoy the children's sack race during the 2012 Braemar Highland Gathering.

70 A peaceful moment during a family picnic in the grounds of Balmoral in September 1960, with a baby Prince Andrew on his father's knee being admired by Charles and Anne.

ELIZABETH THE WOMAN

Prince Charles at just 5 weeks old, in December 1948. *Opposite page:* Charles's christening portrait, with his grandparents George VI and Queen Elizabeth in December 1948, and as a 3-year-old having fun with mum at Balmoral in September 1952.

Becoming a mum

'I still find it hard to believe that I really have a baby of my own!' Princess Elizabeth became a mother before she became a monarch, and her delight in her young family is obvious from early photographs.

71 Prince Charles was born on 14 November 1948, six days before his parents' first wedding anniversary. Official telegrams from the King's Secretary stated that the baby had been born at 9.14pm. Although the Second World War had been over for three years, the nation was still experiencing post-war food rationing, so the Princess asked for food parcels to be sent to the mothers of every child born in Britain on the same day as her baby.

72 Two weeks after the birth, Princess Elizabeth sent a letter to her cousin, Lady May Cambridge: 'The baby is very sweet, and Philip and I are enormously proud of him. I still find it hard to believe that I really have a baby of my own!'

73 'New joy has come to the Royal Family' proclaimed the Movietone newsreel following Princess Anne's birth on 15 August 1950. Spectators had lined The Mall outside Buckingham Palace for days. While waiting for news of the birth, they were treated to several royal sightings, including Queen Elizabeth arriving for lunch with her daughter, and Prince Philip nipping out to Lords to watch the Test Match. (That August the West Indian cricket team beat England 3–1.)

74 The Queen chose to have her children in two stages, leaving a gap of a decade between her older and younger children. After the birth of Prince Andrew, on 19 February 1960, she wrote to her cousin Lady May Cambridge: 'The baby is adorable, and is very good, and putting on weight well. Both the older children are completely riveted by him, and all in all, he's going to be terribly spoilt by all of us, I'm sure!'

75 The Queen's final child was Prince Edward, born on 10 March 1964, witnessed by his father, who for the first time had been allowed in the delivery

room. On 5 August The Queen wrote to Helen Rowe, the midwife who had assisted at the birth, to say: 'The baby is wonderful – good as gold, trying to sit up and weighing 15lbs 12! He smiles and giggles at everyone, and makes everyone happy.'

76 The Queen has only broken with the tradition of attending the State Opening of Parliament twice during her reign: both times she was pregnant, first with Prince Andrew and then with Prince Edward.

77 Lord Mountbatten once commented that The Queen's favourite night of the week was 'Mabel's night off'. He revealed in an interview that when Mabel Anderson, Prince Charles's and Princess Anne's nanny, was off duty, 'Elizabeth could kneel beside the bath, bathe her babies, read to them and put them to bed herself'.

78 Thousands of people attended Prince
Charles's investiture at Caernarvon
Castle on 1 July 1969. Millions more
watched it on television around the world.
Perhaps The Queen was reminded on that
day of her own coronation. When she had
returned to Buckingham Palace and wearily
removed the heavy Imperial State crown,
the little prince had tried to grab it!

79 Like any mother, The Queen never
stops worrying about her children.
It was with a huge relief that she greeted
Prince Andrew on his safe arrival home from
the Falklands War (right). According to one
royal biographer, The Queen always keeps a
photo of Andrew's return in her handbag.

80 The Queen is a working mother,
needing to separate her duties
from her home life. In 2018, in a BBC
documentary about her coronation, it was
explained that Prince Charles and Princess
Anne stayed at the palace while she was
being crowned. When interviewer Alastair
Bruce asked what the children did on that
day, The Queen replied witheringly, 'I've
no idea, I wasn't there!' This provoked a
Twitter storm of appreciation about the
'sassy' Queen.

The Queen in her own words

The Queen started her public speaking career aged 14, with her first wartime radio broadcast. Her speeches are drafted by many official government writers before being handed to an inner team of editors, although Her Majesty will always have input and add ideas. Her Christmas speeches are her own.

81 'Now I shall give you a description of our dresses. They were white silk with old cream lace and had little gold bows all the way down the middle. They had puffed sleeves with one little bow in the centre. Then there were the robes of purple velvet with gold on the edge.'
From an essay written by Princess Elizabeth about the coronation of her parents in 1937

82 'I want to talk to all the little boys and girls who are listening in. And I want to say just this to you – there's nothing at all to be frightened about...'
From Princess Elizabeth's wartime speech on Children's Hour, *October 1940.*

Electronics can't create comradeship; computers can't generate compassion; satellites can't transmit tolerance

83 'On my 21st birthday I welcome the opportunity to speak to all the people of the British Commonwealth and Empire ... This is a happy day for me, but it is also one which brings serious thoughts, thoughts of life looming ahead with all its challenges and with all its opportunity.'
Cape Town, 21 April 1947.

84 'I have in sincerity pledged myself to your service, as so many of you are pledged to mine. Throughout all my life and with all my heart I shall strive to be worthy of your trust.'
Excerpt from The Queen's Coronation Speech, 2 June 1953.

85 'Mastery of technology may blind us to the more fundamental needs of people. Electronics can't create comradeship; computers can't generate compassion; satellites can't transmit tolerance.' *Christmas Day broadcast 1983.*

86 'I think Mr Deng would be happier if he was allowed to smoke.'
The Queen to Foreign Secretary Sir Geoffrey Howe, observing the chain-smoking Chinese leader's obvious discomfort at an official banquet, 1986.

Throughout all my life and with all my heart I shall strive to be worthy of your trust.

*In good times and bad, she never lost her capacity to smile and laugh, nor to inspire others with her warmth and kindness …
No one who knew
Diana well will ever forget her.*

87 'It is possible to have too much of a good thing. A well-meaning Bishop was obviously doing his best when he told Queen Victoria, "Ma'am, we cannot pray too often, nor too fervently, for the Royal Family". The Queen's reply was: "Too fervently, no; too often, yes". I, like Queen Victoria, have always been a believer in that old maxim "moderation in all things".'
24 November 1992, at the Guildhall in London, on the 40th anniversary of her succession.

88 'She was an exceptional and gifted human being. In good times and bad, she never lost her capacity to smile and laugh, nor to inspire others with her warmth and kindness … No one who knew Diana well will ever forget her.'
5 September 1997, following the death of Diana, Princess of Wales.

89 'When people in 53 years from now look back on us, they will doubtless view many of our practices as old-fashioned. But it is my hope that, when judged by future generations, our sincerity, our willingness to take a lead and our determination to do the right thing will stand the test of time.'
Addressing the UN General Assembly in July 2010.

I, like Queen Victoria, have always been a believer in that old maxim 'moderation in all things'

90 During a Privy Council meeting in 2002, Cabinet Minister Clare Short's mobile phone could be heard ringing in her handbag. Obviously, she ignored the phone call, which prompted The Queen to tease her, 'Oh dear, I hope it wasn't anyone important'.

As a younger woman, The Queen was an active equestrian, as seen here at Royal Ascot in 1961.

Opposite page:
The Queen is never without a trusty Launer handbag, or a smile on race day as she shares a joke with winning jockey Frankie Dettori at Ascot in 1999.

A few of Her Majesty's favourite things

Famously fond of riding, breeding and racing horses, The Queen never appears happier than when watching her thoroughbreds compete, or when surrounded by a tumbling bundle of royal corgis.

91 The Queen's lifelong love of horses began on her fourth birthday, when her grandfather George V gave her a Shetland pony named Peggy. The young Princess declared, 'If I am ever Queen, I shall make a law that there must be no riding on Sundays. Horses should have a rest too.'

92 As a child, Princess Elizabeth's favourite books were *Moorland Mousie* (1929) by Muriel Wallace (written under the pseudonym Golden Gorse) and *Black Beauty* (1877) by Anna Sewell. Both are stories about horses, and in both the importance of being kind to animals is paramount.

93 The Queen only uses handbags made by English company Launer, who hold a Royal Warrant. She has over 200 colours and styles, although it's said that she favours the *Traviata* and the *Royale*.

94 As part of her careful diet, The Queen avoids too many carbohydrates, although she loves chocolate. Australians were thrilled to learn that she is a fan of famous Aussie cake, the Lamington (squares of sponge dipped in chocolate and coconut).

95 The Queen has admitted publicly that, unlike her mother, she is not a 'hands-on' gardener, but that she loves spending time in her gardens. John Anderson, Keeper of the gardens at Frogmore House, has said that The Queen is fond of wild flowers, and that her favourite flower is the primrose. In a 2018 ITV documentary, *The Queen's Green Planet*, Her Majesty spoke to Sir David Attenborough of her lifelong love of trees. She has put her name to 'The Queen's Commonwealth Canopy', a project to create a global network of protected forests, actively supported by younger members of the Royal Family.

This page: (**below left**) **Compo, Cleggy and Norman in BBC sitcom** *Last of the Summer Wine.* (**Below right**) **The Queen enjoying one of her favourite hobbies on safari in 1950. (Bottom) Dubonnet and gin, The Queen's tipple of choice?**

Opposite page: **The Queen with corgis in tow as she arrives at Aberdeen airport for a holiday at Balmoral in 1974.**

96 When the actor Peter Sallis received an OBE from The Queen in 2007, she revealed to him that she loved watching the television series that made him famous, *Last of the Summer Wine*. The British sitcom premiered in 1973 and ran for 31 series until 2010.

97 In 1989 the only colour of nail polish that The Queen would wear was a pale pink named 'Ballet Slippers' made by Essie. Her hairdresser wrote that it was her favourite 'because it goes with everything'.

98 Dubonnet (sweet red vermouth) and gin has been widely reported to be The Queen's favourite cocktail. A recipe for how to make this tipple appeared in newspapers all over the world, and suggests two parts of Dubonnet to one part Gordon's gin, with ice and a slice of lemon.

99 The Queen is a keen photographer, and enjoys taking pictures and moving images of her family. She used a movie camera to capture moments on her tour of the Commonwealth with Prince Philip, and has used one on many of her travels ever since.

100 Dookie, a Pembroke Welsh Corgi bought by George VI in 1933, was the first of a long line of royal corgis. The Queen has owned over 30 corgis during her reign, as well as other breeds of dogs. On her 18th birthday, Princess Elizabeth was given a corgi she named Susan. Susan went on honeymoon with the Princess and was destined to become the matriarch of a royal dynasty. When Susan came into season while the couple was staying at Balmoral, she was flown to the breeder in London – on a Royal Mail plane – to be mated with a stud dog named Lucky Strike.

Queen and countryside

Dogs, horses, fresh air and informality – the perfect antidotes to the decorum and pressure of life on royal duty. It's obvious from photographs taken throughout her life how much The Queen loves the countryside, particularly when on the Balmoral Estate, Scotland.

101 Queen Elizabeth and Princesses Elizabeth (left) and Margaret return from a picnic to celebrate Margaret's 21st birthday at Balmoral in August 1951.

103 The Braemer Gathering (tartan essential!) is an annual royal treat.

104 Dancing an eightsome reel with Prince Philip in Edinburgh in 1982.

102 The Queen striding out during Gun Dog Trials in Scotland in 1967.

105 The Queen and Princess Margaret up early for an invigorating morning ride with the Duke of Beaufort in April 1959.

106 The Queen and Prince Philip enjoy a stroll to a farm on the Balmoral Estate in 1972.

107 The Queen rides out above Balmoral during the Royal Family's annual holiday in September 1971.

108 The Queen with her black labradors in Scotland in 1972.

109 The Queen chats to winner Douglas Walker after presenting him with the Challenge Cup at the Retriever Trials in Scotland, 1967.

110 The Queen rests with her corgis at the beautiful Garbh Alt burn in Scotland in 1971.

ELIZABETH THE WIFE, MOTHER, GRANDMOTHER AND GREAT-GRANDMOTHER

In 1947 Princess Elizabeth announced her engagement to naval officer Philip Mountbatten. Their wedding later that year dispelled some of Britain's post-war gloom, while the young, radiant bride and handsome groom captured the hearts of a nation. It was not all smooth sailing for Prince Philip as he had to relinquish a promising naval career to support The Queen, but he eventually carved out a role for himself at her side. Their four children – Prince Charles and Princess Anne born before and Princes Andrew and Edward after the coronation – have also given them the huge pleasure of grandchildren and great-grandchildren and, as in every family, some sadness. Prince Philip has supported her throughout it all, and The Queen's gratitude to her 'strength and stay' was tenderly expressed on their platinum wedding anniversary in 2017.

Prince Philip and Princess Elizabeth with ta young Charles and Anne in the grounds of their London home, Clarence House, in August 1951.

I, Elizabeth Alexandra Mary, take thee…

Two thousand wedding invitations were sent out for one of the most eagerly awaited weddings of the century. The happy couple received around 2,500 presents from all over the world. The official wedding cake (there were 12 in all) was 9ft high and weighed 500lb!

111 Many designers submitted designs for Princess Elizabeth's wedding dress, but Norman Hartnell emerged triumphant when one of his 12 drawings was chosen. There were only three months until the wedding, so 350 dressmakers set to work on the dress. It took them seven weeks to complete.

112 With appropriate tact in a nervous post-war world, Hartnell ordered the silk satin needed for the dress from a Scottish firm. But questions were still asked – where had the actual silkworms come from? Surely not from Japan, a former enemy? Hartnell confirmed that they were 'Chinese worms – from Nationalist China' and that those used to make the silk for the train were English – hailing from Kent.

Norman Hartnell.

This page: **(below)** Rationing-beating cake ingredients arrive in 1947 from the Girl Guides of Australia. **(Right)** The finishing touches are made to the 9ft high 'official' wedding cake.

Opposite page: **(top)** The wedding party. Princess Elizabeth had eight bridesmaids, including her sister, Princess Margaret, who is standing next to Prince Philip. **(Bottom)** Despite the poor weather, people waited for hours to see the happy couple go past.

113 Princess Elizabeth famously saved up her clothing ration coupons for her wedding dress. She was also allotted an extra 100 ration coupons for her special day and her bridesmaids and page-boys were also given extra clothing coupons.

114 A celebratory ball was held before the wedding, at which – it was later revealed – the bride's father, King George VI, was at the head of a conga line, which snaked through all the State Rooms at Buckingham Palace.

115 The wedding took place on 20 November 1947, a bright moment in a Britain ravaged by war. The ceremony, at Westminster Abbey, was broadcast live on radio to 42 countries. It was also filmed and shown on BBC Television that evening; some time later it was also shown on television stations around the world.

116 The Princess was the tenth member of the modern Royal Family to be married at Westminster Abbey. Other royal weddings celebrated there included that of her parents in 1923.

117 The Princess had eight bridesmaids – HRH Princess Margaret, The Hon. Margaret Elphinstone (later Margaret Rhodes), The Hon. Pamela Mountbatten, Lady Mary Cambridge, HRH Princess Alexandra of Kent, Lady Caroline Montagu-Douglas-Scott, Lady Elizabeth Lambart and The Hon. Diana Bowes-Lyon (the Princess's first cousin) – and two page-boys, Prince William of Gloucester and Prince Michael of Kent.

118 The bridal bouquet, provided by the Worshipful Company of Gardeners, was composed of white orchids and a sprig of myrtle. The inclusion of myrtle is a royal wedding tradition. It is always taken from a bush that was grown from the myrtle used in Queen Victoria's wedding bouquet. After the wedding The Queen laid her bouquet on the Tomb of the Unknown Soldier in Westminster Abbey; her mother had done the same.

119 As the bride was one of the most famous Girl Guides in the world, it was fitting that some of the ingredients used to make her official wedding cake were donated by Australian Guides. Instead of being eaten at the wedding reception, slices of the 12 wedding cakes were sent to charities, as well as to schoolchildren and patients and staff at hospitals throughout the country.

120 The Prince and Princess spent the first part of their

honeymoon at Broadlands House in Hampshire, owned by the Duke's uncle, Lord Mountbatten, before travel to Balmoral. They left the wedding in an open-topped landau, which drove past the cheering crowds to Victoria Station. The new bride wore a going-away dress and coat in powder blue, made by Norman Hartnell.

Philip, Prince Consort

Princess Elizabeth was determined to marry her handsome naval officer; what was less clear to him was the role he was to play once he relinquished his naval career to support his wife, the future queen.

121 Prince Philippos of Greece and Denmark was born on 10 June 1921, on the island of Corfu. His mother, Princess Alice of Battenberg, gave birth to him on the family's dining table! His father, Prince Andrea, was absent, fighting in the army. He did not meet his son for several months. When Prince Philip was 18 months old, his family fled from war-torn Greece to France.

122 As a young boy, Philip was sent to England to go to boarding school. His first school was Cheam in Surrey. Later he was educated briefly at a school in Germany – where his married sisters lived – before being sent back to Britain to attend Gordonstoun in Scotland.

123 Princess Elizabeth met Prince Philip several times during childhood, but the most memorable time was when she was 13 years old. It was July 1939, shortly before the outbreak of the Second World War, and she and her sister were touring the Royal Naval College at Dartmouth with her parents. Eighteen-year-old Prince Philip was one of the naval cadets. After the tour, he was invited to join the two Princesses for tea and biscuits.

124 By the time war was declared, Prince Philip was a midshipman in the Royal Navy. During the War he served on ships around the North Sea, the Mediterranean and the Indian and Pacific Oceans. In 1941 he fought notably in the Battle of Matapan, for which he was awarded the Greek War Cross for Valour.

Opposite page: **Newly weds Princess Elizabeth and the Duke of Edinburgh pose for the press in the grounds of Broadlands, home of the Earl of Mountbatten.**

This page: **(left) Sikor Natuan, son of the local chief of Yaohnanen, displays two official portraits of Prince Philip. (Below) The Prince accompanies The Queen in 1976 as she opens the National Theatre's new home on London's South Bank.**

125 On 9 July 1947 the royal engagement was announced. The groom-to-be had been born with the German-sounding surname of Schleswig-Holstein-Sonderburg-Glücksburg. In post-war Britain this was something of a liability, so it was changed to Mountbatten – from his maternal grandparents – before the happy announcement was made. Shortly before the wedding he was given the title of His Royal Highness The Duke of Edinburgh.

126 At the start of his marriage, Prince Philip was still a serving naval officer. In the autumn of 1949 he was posted to Malta as second-in-command of the destroyer HMS *Chequers*. When Princess Elizabeth joined him they lived in the Villa Guardamangia, which had been rented by Prince Philip's uncle Lord Mountbatten. In 1950 Prince Philip was given command of the HMS *Magpie*.

127 The Prince had to give up his promising naval career in order to support his wife. As The Queen's cousin Margaret Rhodes observed, 'It was a very difficult position for a man like him, very bright mentally, to accept that you're always going to walk a couple of paces behind your wife. There was no role model

– the Prince Consort was a totally different kettle of fish – so he had to carve out a career for himself. He has done miraculously well.'

128 On their 60th wedding anniversary in November 1997, The Queen said of her husband: 'All too often, I fear, Prince Philip has had to listen to me speaking. Frequently we have discussed my intended speech beforehand and, as you will imagine, his views have been expressed in a forthright manner. He is someone who doesn't take easily to compliments but he has, quite simply, been my strength and stay all these years, and I, and his whole family, and this and many other countries, owe him a debt greater than he would ever claim, or we shall ever know.'

129 '[Philip] is much mellower in his older age but there is still a spark of rebellion lying in wait, ready to pounce, which is rather refreshing....' Margaret Rhodes, in an interview for the *Daily Telegraph*, just before Prince Philip's 90th birthday in 2011.

130 Whatever his personal sacrifices in his loyal support of wife and country, Prince Philip is still regarded as nothing less than a god to members of a tribal cult on the South Pacific Island of Vanuatu. Members of the cult pray to him daily, asking for his blessing. In answer to their requests, worshippers on Vanuatu have been sent several photographs of the Prince over the years, including one that shows him holding a club which the tribe made for him.

ELIZABETH THE WIFE, MOTHER, GRANDMOTHER AND GREAT-GRANDMOTHER

49

The Queen's children as adults

The Queen's four children – HRH Prince Charles, HRH Princess Anne The Princess Royal, HRH Prince Andrew, Duke of York, and HRH Prince Edward, Earl of Wessex, have pursued different interests as adults. They have all had to face challenges in combining their private lives with public royal duties as they support The Queen.

131 **Prince Charles** was the first heir to the throne to be sent to school, the first to take public exams, one of the few to go to university (Cambridge) and to gain a degree before entering the military, where he served in all three armed forces, retiring from active service in 1976 to take up public duties.

132 One of his major contributions to public life has been the Prince's Trust, which he started as a small, private charity after hearing a radio broadcast about deprived young people in Britain. Using his own money, he helped various youth schemes anonymously and discreetly until he was persuaded to go public. The Trust was launched formally in December 1976, and The Queen granted it a Royal Charter in 1999. It is now one of the most important charities in Britain, and includes a business start-up scheme for young people.

133 Charles's concerns about the environment first surfaced when he was a teenager, long before they became fashionable. The Prince is passionate about many things, from organic farming to modern architecture, and as heir to the throne is sometimes criticised for 'overstepping the line' between personal opinion and official impartiality.

134 A highly eligible bachelor until he was 30, Charles married the 19-year-old Diana Spencer in 1981. The marriage was dissolved in 1996; a year later, the Princess was tragically killed in a car crash in Paris. In 2005 Charles married Camilla Parker Bowles. The couple support many charities and perform public duties together and separately.

135 Known as the 'hardest working royal', **Princess Anne** (The Queen made her Princess Royal in 1987) is respected as a tireless advocate for charity, in particular Save the Children, of which

138 Unlike his brothers, Prince Andrew, Duke of York did not go to university but left school to train as a Royal Naval Officer. After passing out he learnt to fly helicopters and served on HMS *Invincible* during the Falklands War of 1983. When he left the Royal Navy after 22 years he was appointed UK Special Representative for Trade and Development. He resigned from this role in 2011, following criticism of his friendships with controversial figures. Andrew married childhood friend Sarah Ferguson, nicknamed 'Fergie', in 1986; the couple separated in 1993 and divorced in 1996. He now supports many charities and is the Chair of the Outward Bound Trust.

139 The Queen's youngest son, Prince Edward, Earl of Wessex (he chose the title, inspired by a Shakespearean character) was born in 1964. He studied history at Cambridge, where he enjoyed performing in and producing several student shows. After college, Edward joined the Royal Marines, but dropped out of training in favour of a career in entertainment. His first venture was the Grand Knockout Tournament in 1987, in which several royals took part. Their televised performances were considered rather undignified; however, the show raised over £1m for charity.

she became President in 1970. She is also closely involved with the Princess Royal's Trust for Carers, and around 200 other charities.

136 The Princess is an excellent equestrian, specialising in three-day eventing, and she is admired for her physical stamina. Despite having recently recovered from an abdominal operation, she won gold in the European Championships in 1971 on her horse Doublet, a present from The Queen. Anne also competed in the 1976 Montreal Olympics, and although she was concussed in a fall the day before, she jumped a clear round, just missing out on a medal.

137 Anne married fellow equestrian Captain Mark Phillips in 1973; the couple had two children Peter and Zara, before the marriage was dissolved in April 1992. In December that year she married Commander (now Vice Admiral) Timothy Laurence of the Royal Navy. Anne was the first royal since Henry VIII to divorce and remarry.

140 In 1988 Prince Edward joined the Really Useful Theatre Group founded by Andrew Lloyd Webber; five years later he founded his own television company, Ardent Films. Edward married PR executive Sophie Rhys Jones in 1999. The Prince left Ardent Films in 2002 to support The Queen in her Golden Jubilee year; Sophie also relinquished her business interests. Both now work to support many charities, and Edward often travels abroad to represent The Queen and on behalf of the Foreign Office.

Grandchildren and great-grandchildren

Her Majesty Queen Elizabeth II, Head of the Commonwealth, Defender of the Faith… also known as 'Gan Gan'.

141 The Queen and the Duke of Edinburgh first became grandparents when Princess Anne had a son, Peter Phillips. Obligingly, Peter arrived in 1977 – the year of his grandmother's Silver Jubilee. Four years later his sister, Zara, was born.

142 Prince William, the eldest child of Prince Charles and Princess Diana, was born in 1982. When William was very little, he was unable to say the word 'Granny', so instead he called The Queen 'Gary'. This caused great confusion for guests at Buckingham Palace when the little prince fell over and sobbed for 'Gary' – the guests assumed he was calling for a member of the household staff.

143 Prince William's younger brother, Prince Henry, was born in 1984. He is known as Prince 'Harry', and is renowned for his cheeky sense of humour. He served in the British Army for ten years, in the Blues and Royals; his career included serving in the war in Afghanistan. In 2018 Harry married his American girlfriend, the actress Meghan Markle.

144 Princesses Beatrice (born 1988) and Eugenie (born 1990) are the daughters of Prince Andrew and Sarah, Duchess of York. In 2016 Prince Andrew wrote proudly, 'As a father, my wish for my daughters is for them to be modern working young women, who happen to be Members of the Royal Family, and I am delighted to see them building their careers'.

145 Prince Edward and his wife Sophie, Countess of Wessex, have two children: Lady Louise Windsor (born 2003) and James, Viscount Severn (born 2007). Their parents asked for their children not to be known as princess and prince, in the hopes they could have a more 'normal' life than their royal cousins.

146 There was great excitement when William and Catherine, the Duke and Duchess of Cambridge, had their first baby. Their son, Prince George of Cambridge, was born in 2013, and his sister, Princess Charlotte, was born two years later. The 2013 change in the rules on royal succession means that male royal children no longer take precedence, so Charlotte is fourth in line to the throne. In 2018 her brother Prince Louis was born. He is fifth in line to the throne, taking precedence over his uncle Prince Harry.

Portrait of The Queen taken by Annie Leibovitz in 2016, with her five great-grandchildren and her two youngest grandchildren, in the Green Drawing Room at Windsor Castle. The children are (from bottom left): Mia Tindall (holding The Queen's handbag), 2-year-old daughter of Zara and Mike Tindall; James, Viscount Severn (aged 8) and Lady Louise (12), children of the Earl and Countess of Wessex and the youngest of The Queen's eight grandchildren; Savannah (5) and Isla Phillips (3), daughters of The Queen's eldest grandson, Peter Phillips and his wife, Autumn; Prince George (2) and, on The Queen's lap, her (then) youngest great-grandchild, Princess Charlotte (11 months), children of The Duke and Duchess of Cambridge. Prince Louis, born on 23 April 2018, is currently The Queen's youngest great-grandson.

147 When The Queen's grandson Peter Phillips met Canadian Autumn Kelly, he knew it was love at first sight, but *she* had no idea he was a royal until she spotted him on television, standing next to his cousin Prince William! Peter and Autumn married in 2008, and presented The Queen with more great-grandchildren. Savannah was born in 2010, followed by her sister Isla in 2012.

148 In 2013 Zara Tindall (née Phillips) gave birth to her first child, a daughter named Mia who is currently the second youngest of The Queen's great-granddaughters. Sport is in the Tindall children's blood: their mother is a professional showjumper and their father, Mike Tindall, is a professional rugby player.

149 The Queen's most prominent grandsons, Princes William and Harry, have grown into young men who represent a new, more accessible, generation of royals. They are refreshingly open about their emotional struggle to deal with the sudden death of their mother, Princess Diana, and in doing so have helped create more public awareness of depression. In 2017 the Princes, together with the Duchess of Cambridge, launched a new mental health campaign, 'Heads Together'.

150 Out of the mouths of babes... In an interview to mark The Queen's 90th birthday, the Duchess of Cambridge revealed that her son, Prince George, calls his great-grandmother 'Gan Gan'.

'My strength and stay'

This was how The Queen described her husband, during a speech to mark their golden wedding anniversary in 1997, adding: '… I owe him a debt greater than he would ever claim, or we shall ever know.'

151 The Queen and Prince Philip remain united after over 70 years together.

152 In 2017 The Queen and Prince Philip became the first royal couple to celebrate a platinum wedding anniversary. Their official portrait is a photograph by Matt Holyoake, which shows the couple standing between two paintings by Thomas Gainsborough, of King George III and Queen Charlotte. On 20 November 2017 the bells of Westminster Abbey were rung to celebrate the royal couple's 70 years of marriage.

153 The Queen filming from the deck of the HMS *Gothic* during the coronation world tour of 1953, with Prince Philip not far behind.

154 The Queen and Prince Philip chat during a musical performance in the Abbey Gardens, Bury St Edmunds, in July 2002.

155 Sharing their love of racing, the royal couple follow racehorses in 1968.

158 The Duke and Princess Elizabeth on board the destroyer *Crusader* bound for British Columbia during the Commonwealth tour of 1951.

156 The Prince accompanies The Queen to the State Opening of Parliament in 2004.

159 The Queen and Prince Philip at a service in St Paul's Cathedral in 2017 to mark the centenary of the Order of the British Empire.

157 In May 1956 polo was one of Prince Philip's favourite pastimes, and the family came along too!

160 Party wind down – The Queen and Prince Philip return from the first of the Royal Garden Parties of 2011 (see also page 76).

Sadness and loss

During The Queen's long life and reign she has, inevitably, suffered many personal sorrows, including the premature death of her father. Harder still, she has also had to endure them in full, and sometimes critical, public gaze.

161 The Queen's father, George VI, died at Sandringham House on 6 February 1952, after serving for 15 years as monarch. The cause of death was coronary thrombosis, although the King had been suffering from lung cancer and arteriosclerosis. In 1951 he underwent an operation to remove a lung but the cancer was not beaten. He was found by his valet, dead in his bed at 7.30am; the official announcement from Sandringham was delivered at 10.45am.

162 The new Queen Elizabeth II was on a royal tour in Kenya when her father died; she was informed as rapidly as possible and attempted to fly straight home, but a thunderstorm delayed her flight. She arrived to widespread public mourning, with more than 300,000 people queueing to see her father's coffin lying in state in Westminster Hall.

163 In 1972 The Queen, together with Prince Philip and Prince Charles, visited her uncle the Duke of Windsor and his wife, the Duchess, at their home in France. It was 36 years after his abdication. The former almost-king looked very ill and thin, although he told The Queen when she asked after his health that he was 'not so bad'. Ten days later he was dead.

164 In 1978 The Queen was saddened by the news that her sister, Princess Margaret, was to divorce her husband, Lord Snowdon. The Queen and the Duke of Edinburgh have also had to endure their three older children, Prince Charles, Princess Anne and Prince Andrew, coping with their divorces.

165 In August 1979 the family suffered a terrible loss when Earl Mountbatten of Burma was murdered by the IRA. The bomb planted on his boat also killed four other people, including his 14-year-old grandson Nicholas.

Members of the Irish Guard bear the Queen Mother's coffin, adorned with camellias from her own garden and draped in her own personal standard, in April 2002.

166 On the night of 31 August 1997 Princess Diana and her lover Dodi Al-Fayed were killed in a car crash in Paris. The Queen and other senior members of the Royal Family were criticised widely in the media for not

showing enough emotion in public. What few people noticed at the funeral, however, was the way in which The Queen broke with accepted protocol and bowed her head to her daughter-in-law's coffin, as it passed her. Since this extraordinary outpouring of

2002, at the age of 71, after a series of strokes, was a time of great personal sadness for The Queen.

168 Queen Elizabeth The Queen Mother died on 30 March 2002, at the age of 101, just weeks after the death of her younger daughter. Buckingham Palace announced that she 'died peacefully in her sleep at 3.15 this afternoon at Royal Lodge'. Queen Elizabeth II, still in mourning for her sister, was at her mother's bedside.

169 In 2003 Sophie, Countess of Wessex, went into a terrifying premature labour with her first child. The baby was in distress and the countess needed an emergency caesarean. It happened so fast that Prince Edward was unable to get to the hospital before his daughter, Louise, was born. Sophie lost so much blood that she almost died, and baby Louise weighed only 4lb 9oz. As a result of her prematurity Louise suffered from the eye condition strabismus. Mother and baby rallied, and are now both healthy. The Countess campaigns to help alleviate the plight of children with sight issues.

170 Of the many atrocities that occurred during The Queen's reign, the IRA nail bombs of 1982 that targeted soldiers and horses near to Buckingham Palace were particularly horrific. As soldiers from the Royal Household Cavalry rode through Hyde Park for the Changing of The Guard, a 25-lb nail bomb was detonated, killing and hideously maiming men and animals. Two hours later another bomb went off in Regents Park, near the bandstand, where men from the Royal Green Jackets were playing. In total, 11 soldiers and seven horses were killed and many other people were badly injured. A black horse, Sefton, became the icon of that day. Despite terrible injuries he survived and returned to military duties, as a hero.

public grief, many members of the Royal Family have felt able to abandon the pretence of the British 'stiff upper lip'. The change in the way The Queen has behaved in public ever since has been welcomed and much admired.

167 The Queen has always been very close to her younger sister; at many times in her life, Princess Margaret was one of the few people who could really understand what The Queen was going through. Her death on 9 February

ELIZABETH THE WIFE, MOTHER, GRANDMOTHER AND GREAT-GRANDMOTHER

ELIZABETH THE SOVEREIGN

E lizabeth was just 25 when she became queen in 1952. Her coronation the following year, the first ever to be televised, contributed to making her arguably the world's most famous monarch. Her Christmas speeches, first televised in 1957, have become a British tradition. She has received thousands of diplomatic gifts and met hundreds of other world leaders at glittering functions. At one time patron of over 600 charities, The Queen has done more for charity than any other monarch in history. Over her long reign, The Queen has inspired works of music, costume design, new dishes and poetry. In her poem 'The Crown', written to celebrate the 60th anniversary of the coronation, poet laureate Carol Anne Duffy echoed Her Majesty's own words: 'My whole life, whether it be long or short, devoted to your service.'

Queen Elizabeth II, wearing the Imperial State Crown, leaves Westminster Abbey in the Gold State Coach after her coronation in 1953.

'All this – and Everest too!'

After 16 months of preparation, The Queen's coronation took place on 2 June 1953. Westminster Abbey had been turned into a vast theatre, so that guests could witness the glittering spectacle, and to top off a perfect day, mountaineer Edmund Hillary reached the summit of Everest!

171 The date of the coronation had been chosen by meteorologists, who with their usual flair predicted fine weather. In the event, after London had sweltered for days, 2 June dawned cold, grey and rainy in London.

172 On the day of the coronation, the news arrived that Edmund Hillary, a New Zealander taking part in a British expedition to Mount Everest, had become the first recorded person to reach the summit. The banner headline on the coronation edition of the *Daily Express* read: 'All this – and Everest too!'

173 Queen Elizabeth II was only the sixth British queen to be crowned in Westminster Abbey as the monarch (as opposed to being crowned as a queen consort, the wife of a king). The very first British queen to be crowned in her own right was Queen Mary I, whose coronation took place exactly four centuries previously, in 1553.

Opposite page: **(left)
The Queen arriving at
Westminster Abbey for
her coronation in 1953.
(Right) Some onlookers
in the vast crowds found
a better view!**

This page: **(left) A very
young Prince Charles
watches his mother
crowned Queen, with
his grandmother and
aunt. (Right) A treasured
souvenir of the event.**

174 The coronation bouquet was
composed of all-white flowers.
It represented the United Kingdom, with
English lilies-of-the-valley, carnations from
Northern Ireland and the Isle of Man,
Welsh orchids, and stephanotis from
Scotland.

175 The Duke of Edinburgh arrived
at Westminster Abbey in his
naval uniform, but for the coronation itself
he wore his ducal robe over his uniform.
He also wore a coronet.

176 The coronation procession
comprised 250 people. These
included the Yeoman of the Guard,
politicians, church leaders, civil servants,
members of the Royal Household, and
political leaders from all over the
Commonwealth.

177 One of the most sacred parts of
the coronation is the anointing
of the new monarch by the Archbishop of
Canterbury. The precious oil – made from
extracts of roses, oranges, musk,
cinnamon and ambergris – usually lasts
for decades. However, a new batch had to
be created for The Queen, as the previous
vial had been destroyed during a wartime
bombing raid.

PUBLISHED BY GRACIOUS PERMISSION OF
HER MAJESTY THE QUEEN

THE CORONATION
OF HER MAJESTY
QUEEN
ELIZABETH II
APPROVED SOUVENIR PROGRAMME

KING GEORGE'S 2/6 JUBILEE TRUST

KING GEORGE'S JUBILEE TRUST

APPROVED SOUVENIR CORONATION PROGRAMME

BOY SCOUT SELLER

178 Hundreds of thousands of well-wishers waited in the rain to watch the coronation procession. Many of them had camped out on the pavements overnight. Queen Salote of Tonga won people's hearts by refusing to close the roof of her carriage against the rain, continuing to smile and wave to the cheering crowds as she passed.

179 The coronation was held a few days before the Derby, in which The Queen's horse, Aureole, was due to run. While helping The Queen dress for the coronation ceremony, one of her maids of honour commented that she must be nervous, to which The Queen reportedly replied, 'Of course I am, but I really think Aureole will win.' Her (deliberate?) misunderstanding has been interpreted in several ways, but it's just possible that she may have been joking to relax everyone else!

180 The Queen wore her stunning coronation dress, designed by Norman Hartnell on several further occasions during her 1952 tour of the Commonwealth. She wore the dress, embellished with national symbols, at state openings of Parliament in Australia, New Zealand and Sri Lanka (then called Ceylon).

Norman Hartnell

Crowns and tiaras

The Queen's crowns and tiaras are mostly inherited, although she has also commissioned a few. Tiaras are worn by The Queen, female members of the Royal Family and some members of the titled aristocracy.

181 **The Imperial State Crown, 1937** This crown, made for George VI's coronation, was worn by The Queen at the end of her coronation service in 1953 (see also page 63). It has been used throughout her reign for the State Opening of Parliament.

182 **St Edward's Crown, 1661** (above) Made for the coronation of King Charles II, this crown of solid gold and semi-precious stones is only ever used for the act of crowning the sovereign.

183 **Queen Mary's Girls of Great Britain and Ireland Tiara, 1893** (right, main picture) Known informally as 'Granny's tiara', it was presented to the future Queen Mary as a wedding gift from the 'Girls of Great Britain and Ireland'. She gave it to her granddaughter, Princess Elizabeth (here wearing it in a portrait by Karsh), when she was married in 1947.

184 **The Diamond Diadem, 1820** (right, top) The Queen wore this diadem on her way to her coronation in 1952. It was made for George IV's use at his coronation and has been worn by queens consort and regnant. Queen Victoria wears it in this 1838 portrait by Thomas Sully.

185 The Vladimir Tiara, c1874
(left, centre) Made for the Grand Duchess Marie Pavlovna, this magnificent tiara was smuggled out of Russia during the Russian Revolution and later sold to Queen Mary (here wearing it in this 1935 portrait by Vandyke) before The Queen inherited it.

186 Queen Mary's Fringe Tiara, 1919
(left) Russian-style jewellery was popular among members of the Royal Family in the early 20th century, when this tiara was made for Queen Mary. She gave it to Queen Elizabeth in 1936 (here wearing it in this Dorothy Wilding portrait), who lent it to Princess Elizabeth for her wedding day. The Queen inherited it in 2002.

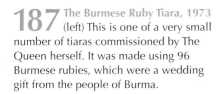

187 The Burmese Ruby Tiara, 1973 (left) This is one of a very small number of tiaras commissioned by The Queen herself. It was made using 96 Burmese rubies, which were a wedding gift from the people of Burma.

188 Queen Elizabeth's Halo Tiara, 1936 (above) This exquisite tiara was worn by the Duchess of Cambridge on her wedding day in 2011 (see also page 138). Made by Cartier, it was presented to The Queen Mother by her husband before their wedding, and then given to Princess Elizabeth on her 18th birthday.

189 The Oriental Tiara, 1853 (above right) A favourite of The Queen Mother's (here wearing it in a Cecil Beaton portrait [detail]), who gave it to Princess Elizabeth. Prince Albert designed this tiara for Queen Victoria. It was originally set with opals; Victoria's daughter-in-law, Queen Alexandra, replaced these with rubies when the tiara was passed to her.

190 The Brazilian Aquamarine Tiara (right) This striking tiara was commissioned by The Queen in 1957 to match a necklace and a pair of earrings presented to her in 1953 as a coronation gift from the people of Brazil. It was enlarged in 1971 to incorporate extra Brazilian aquamarines given to The Queen on her first state visit to Brazil in 1968.

If it's good enough for The Queen...

A Royal Warrant of appointment is a mark of recognition for companies and tradespeople who have supplied goods and services to the most senior royals – The Queen, the Duke of Edinburgh and the Prince of Wales – for at least five years. The warrants featured here were all granted by The Queen herself.

191 In 2008 Her Majesty granted a new Royal Warrant to her favourite umbrella company, Fulton, founded in 1956, in addition to the one they held previously from the Queen Mother. The Queen is a fan of the transparent 'Fulton Birdcage' as it provides weather protection while allowing her to be seen at public events.

192 Brush with fame: the Nash family has been making traditional besom brooms for three centuries, gaining The Queen's Royal Warrant in 1999. The firm has also supplied besom brooms for pagan and traditional Gypsy weddings, to a witchcraft museum and to witches' covens. It also made all the brooms for the *Harry Potter* films.

193 Removals and storage firm Abels first came to the Royal Family's attention in 1981, when they were entrusted with moving presents for newly-wed Prince and Princess of Wales to their new home in Kensington Palace. Seven years later The Queen granted them a Royal Warrant.

194 The Queen has always been interested in the environment and has awarded Royal Warrants to companies that share her interests. These include Agri.Cycle, which specialises in recycling plastic farm waste and spent shotgun cartridges, and Delphis Eco, which manufactures environmentally friendly cleaning products.

195 Palaces and castles frequently require the services of professional chimney sweeps – a job many people think is a thing of the past. The Queen has bestowed Royal Warrants on Milborrow Chimney Sweeps in Sussex, and Kleenway in Berkshire (handily located close to Windsor Castle).

196 Entertaining on a grand scale requires equally lavish lavatories. Event-a-loo, described as a 'Supplier of Executive Toilet Hire', and John Anderson Hire, purveyors of 'VIP loos', both hold Royal Warrants for their temporary luxury loos.

197 Train food seldom has a good press, but Rail Gourmet UK has been granted consecutive Royal Warrants, and has been given the title of Royal Train Caterers. In 2013 a renewed warrant required the company 'to demonstrate its environmental credentials … using only meat and fish from sustainable and accredited sources', as well as carrying out 'rigorous recycling'.

198 The Queen has her very own flag manufacturer; she has also awarded Royal Warrants to picture framers, gilders, and manufacturers of buttons, insignia and medals. There is even a Royal Nosegay Maker: Rosemary Hughes, of Leicestershire, makes all the nosegays carried at the Royal Maundy Service (held annually on the Thursday before Easter Sunday).

199 The Queen's love of animals is reflected in many of the holders

The Queen's umbrella of choice, the see-though 'Fulton Birdcage'.
Left: Scented nosegays, made by Royal Warrant holder Rosemary Hughes, are carried by members of the Royal Family and others taking part in the annual Office of Royal Maundy, when The Queen distributes purse of Maundy money to chosen recipients.

of her Royal Warrant, including several manufacturers of dog and horse food, makers of pet products and equine equipment, farriers, and Bedmax, which manufactures 'bespoke bedding for horses'.

200 Royal Warrants can be taken away. In 2018 the lingerie company Rigby & Peller was stripped of its Royal Warrant, after *Storm in a D Cup* hit the news. The memoir, published by the company's 82-year-old former owner (who was still a member of the board) revealed private conversations and anecdotes. The Queen, the Queen Mother and Princess Diana had all been loyal customers.

Cue... Her Majesty

The Christmas Day speech is the monarch's personal message to the nation and the Commonwealth. The Queen always writes her own speech. On Christmas Day 2015 her broadcast received more TV viewers than any other programme, beating *Downton Abbey* to the top spot.

201 In 1922 BBC executive John Reith suggested to The Queen's grandfather, George V, that he broadcast a Christmas message to the nation. The King wasn't keen; he regarded new-fangled radio as an unsuitable medium for royal use. By 1932 he had changed his mind. His first broadcast was estimated to have reached around 20 million people all over the British Empire.

202 This historic Christmas speech was beautifully crafted for the King by Rudyard Kipling. It began: 'I speak now from my home and from my heart to you all; to men and women so cut off by the snows, the desert, or the sea, that only voices out of the air can reach them.'

203 The decision to broadcast the Christmas message at 3pm was made in the 1930s. The BBC chose the optimum time to reach – via short-wave radio transmitters – as many parts of the British Empire as possible.

204 Perhaps the most memorable Christmas broadcast made by The Queen's father was given in 1939, and no one listening in could fail to understand the gravity of his words: 'A new year is at hand. We cannot tell what it will bring. If it brings peace, how thankful we shall all be. If it brings us continued struggle we shall remain undaunted.'

Opposite page: **(main image) At Her Majesty's suggestion, The Queen's Christmas speech of 2010 was filmed in the Chapel Royal at Hampton Court. (Far left) The future Queen's first experience of live broadcasting came in October 1940, when she and Margaret spoke on 'Children's Hour' in October 1940.**

This page: **(top left) The new Queen makes her first Christmas radio broadcast from Sandringham in 1952. (Bottom left) In 1986, under producer Sir David Attenborough, the speech was filmed in the Royal Mews at Buckingham Palace. (Below) The Queen's first televised Christmas broadcast, in 1957.**

205 The Queen delivered her first Christmas Day radio message to the Commonwealth in 1952. It aired a few minutes late, at 3.07pm. She has delivered a Christmas speech every year of her reign (in 1969 she published instead of broadcasting her speech, because with Prince Charles's investiture and a documentary on the Royal Family it was felt there had been enough television coverage for one year).

206 Her first televised Christmas broadcast, in 1957, was in black and white (colour arrived in 1967). The Queen spoke to camera while seated at her desk, on which Christmas cards and framed photos of her children could be glimpsed.

Her speech was also transmitted via radio, although many listeners complained of US police radio interference, claiming to hear at one point an officer drawl, 'Joe, I'm gonna grab a quick coffee'.

207 Modern royal messages are recorded for TV and radio well in advance of Christmas Day, usually at one of The Queen's residences. In 1975 the speech was filmed outside for the first time, in the gardens of Buckingham Palace.

208 Between 1986 and 1991 the Christmas broadcasts were produced by Sir David Attenborough. His first one showed The Queen in the Royal Mews at Buckingham Palace.

209 In 2010 The Queen suggested a new location at which to record her Christmas message: Hampton Court Palace. She was filmed in the Chapel Royal. Her speech, which featured the anniversary of the King James Bible and the value of sport and teamwork, was intercut with the Chapel Royal choir singing hymns.

210 Unfortunately the public was given advanced notice of the 2010 speech, when *The Sun* newspaper dared to break the time-honoured embargo and published the entire transcript two days early. The Palace began legal proceedings, after which The Queen accepted an apology from the newspaper and £200,000 in damages – which was donated to charity.

ELIZABETH THE SOVEREIGN

Ten diplomatic gifts

The Queen has received a huge variety of official gifts from all over the world: some priceless, some more 'unusual', but all presented with pride.

211 The Queen is presented with a Transport for London roundel for Buckingham Palace at Aldgate Station in 2010.

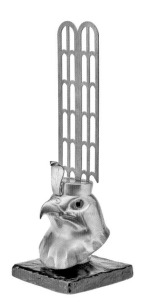

212 A replica of a golden model of Horus, Egyptian god of the sky and kingship, presented in 1991.

213 Reduced-size wooden Nimba shoulder mask, from the Republic of Guinea, 2014.

214 *Vessel of Friendship*, a model of a Chinese treasure ship from the Ming Dynasty, presented in 2015.

215 Mexican Tree of Life for Her Majesty The Queen, presented in 2015.

216 Model of a traditional painted truck from Pakistan, given during The Queen's state visit in 1997.

218 Painted HMs Chogm Chair, with rush seat from Uganda, 2007.

217 Wayang Golek (rod puppet) from Indonesia, presented in 1974.

219 Lapis lazuli bowl, received from the President of Afghanistan in 2007.

220 Silver filigree fan, presented by the President of Paraguay in 1994.

Buffets and banquets

Every year three Royal Garden Parties take place – two at Buckingham Palace in London, and one at the Palace of Holyroodhouse in Edinburgh. And each year The Queen hosts at least one huge formal banquet at Buckingham Palace for a visiting head of state, to which around 700 guests are invited.

Opposite page:
A member of the Queen's Household staff checks that every one of the George IV silver-gilt knives and forks is perfectly placed before a state banquet.

This page: **The Queen and Prince Philip with the President of Ghana, John Agyekumkufuor and his wife at a state banquet at Buckingham Palace in 2007.**

221 State banquets, usually in honour of visiting world leaders, have been held in the Grand Ballroom at Buckingham Palace since 1914. These grand, formal occasions are booked a year in advance, with preparations starting four months ahead of the actual banquet.

222 The horseshoe-shaped table is laid using knives, forks, spoons and salvers from the 4,000-piece silver-gilt Grand Service, bought by George IV over 200 years ago. The finest pieces of the Service are displayed during the meal at the side of the room: a tradition dating from medieval times in which showing finery was a mark of respect to an honoured guest.

223 The crucial organisation of the seating plan is the responsibility of the Master of the Household, who moves around named slips of paper on a large wooden board to craft the perfect arrangement. A great deal of research and thought is put into creating a successful social mix, including noting who has met before and what languages guests can speak.

224 Each place setting is meticulously arranged, with 18 inches between the outside knife and fork. A special measuring stick is used to ensure that each place is uniform. The Queen always does a final check of the completed table a few hours before the banquet.

ELIZABETH THE SOVEREIGN

75

Below: **The Queen** makes a point of personally checking that everything is in order. The tables are so vast that staff have to climb up to arrange the centrepieces.

Bottom: **The Queen with President Obama at the banquet held on the first day of his three-day state visit to Britain in May 2011.**

Right: **Over 30,000** specially invited guests every year enjoy a relaxed afternoon either at one of three garden parties at Buckingham Palace, as seen here, or one at Holyroodhouse House in Scotland.

225 The banquets, normally of three courses, last one hour and 20 minutes. Finally, 12 pipers process around the room, a tradition started by Queen Victoria, before guests rise from the table and move through to the State Rooms for coffee and petit fours. All the washing up of the precious Grand Service and the 18th-century porcelain is done by hand.

226 The garden parties began many years ago as 'presentation parties' for debutantes. The parties were described in 1966 as for 'an elite club for personal friends of royalty', before The Queen instigated changes, extending the

royal invitation to a wider range of people who had made a contribution to society. Today guests are nominated via a large network of associations and institutions and are intended to be 'a representative cross-section of the community'.

227 Women are asked to wear a 'day dress', with hats and gloves optional. Men are advised to wear morning dress, although a 'dark lounge suit' is also acceptable. National dress or military uniform may also be worn. However, as reported in the *Telegraph* in 2008, 'Jeans, sandals and even T-shirts have been seen at recent garden parties'.

228 The Queen attended her first garden party as monarch on 10 July 1952. Among the 7,000 guests was Margaret Truman, the daughter of the US president. Her Majesty wore white organza, and her sister a 'frock of grey lace'.

229 Around 8,000 people attend each royal garden party, from all over the world and, specifically, from all over the Commonwealth. It is estimated that, at a single garden party, 27,000 cups of tea, 20,000 sandwiches and 20,000 cakes are consumed!

230 Despite the elaborate planning, mistakes do happen! In 2011 US President Barack Obama and First Lady Michelle Obama attended a state banquet hosted by The Queen at Buckingham Palace. President Obama was still speaking when the orchestra of the Scots Guards began playing The National Anthem. He continued his speech regardless, which meant he toasted Her Majesty before the anthem had finished. Far from seeming offended, as observers feared, The Queen just smiled and thanked the President for his 'very kind' speech.

'You look like an orchid under cellophane, Your Majesty'

The Queen, *not* in her own words…

231 'The Duke and Duchess, most happy in their own married life, were not over concerned with the higher education of their daughters. They wanted most for them a really happy childhood.' *Marion Crawford,* The Little Princesses *(1950).*

232 In 1936 the Princesses learnt that their father had become king. Margaret Rose asked her sister, 'Does that mean you will have to be the next queen?' 'Yes, some day', replied Elizabeth. 'Poor you!' came the response.

Her uniforms were better tailored than ours, and even her overalls were pressed and laundered every day.

233 A fellow ATS (Auxiliary Territorial Service) member was interviewed by Brian Hoey for his 2006 book *Life with the Queen*. She recalled of the wartime royal recruit: 'Her uniforms were better tailored than ours, and even her overalls were pressed and laundered every day.'

234 'If pushed to say what I like about Elizabeth, who, as I'm sure most of you know, overtook Queen Victoria this week to become our longest-serving monarch, it would be her uncomplaining, getting-on-with ethic.' *Scottish author John Niven, September 2015.*

235 'When I was a little boy, I read about a fairy princess, and there she is'. *President Truman, 1951.*

236 During her tour of Australia in 1954 The Queen was driven around in a limousine covered with a domed clear plastic rainhood so that people could see her as she passed. When she asked her Australian equerry Commander Michael Parker how she appeared, he replied 'You look like an orchid under cellophane, Your Majesty.'

…she loves her duty and means to be a queen and not a puppet.

237 In 1961 British Prime Minister Harold Macmillan rebuffed Parliamentary concerns for The Queen's safety on a proposed visit to Ghana: 'The Queen has been absolutely determined all through. She is grateful for MPs' and press concern about her safety, but she is impatient of the attitude towards her to treat her as a woman, and a film star or mascot. She has indeed "the heart and stomach of a man". She has great faith in the work she can do in the Commonwealth especially … she loves her duty and means to be a queen and not a puppet.'

When I was a little boy, I read about a fairy princess, and there she is.

238 Even Labour MP Richard Crossman, an avowed republican, was a fan of The Queen. After a meeting with her 1966 he wrote: 'She has a lovely laugh. She laughs with her whole face and she just can't assume a mere smile because she's really a very spontaneous person … When she is deeply moved and tries to control it she looks like an angry thunder-cloud. So, very often when she's been deeply touched by the plaudits of the crowd she merely looks terribly bad-tempered.'

We saw your car, Hurrah! Hurrah! We saw you wave, the smile you gave, we saw your horse, of course, of course.

From Christopher Logue's composition The Queen's Birthday Song, *written for Her Majesty's 60th birthday in 1986.*

239 Following the Silver Jubilee Thanksgiving Service at St Paul's Cathedral in June 1977, Lord Mountbatten recorded the following exchange with The Queen: 'I asked her afterwards why she had looked so cross and worried at one time and she laughed and said, "I was just thinking how awful it would be if (Idi) Amin were to gatecrash the party and arrive after all." I asked her what she had proposed to do and she said that she had decided she would use the City's Pearl Sword, which the Lord Mayor had placed in front of her, to hit him hard over the head with.'

When she is deeply moved and tries to control it she looks like an angry thunder-cloud.

240 When interviewed for the documentary *Our Queen At Ninety*, Prince William said of his grandmother: 'A lot of people get very excited and sort of nervous around her. I've seen some very comical moments. I've seen people literally faint in front of her!'

The Queen and her charities

According to the Charities Aid Foundation, Queen Elizabeth II has done more for charity than any other monarch in history. After turning 90 she was advised to reduce her workload, so she passed several of her large number of patronages on to other members of the Royal Family.

241 The Queen is, or has been, patron of more than 600 charities and institutions, including the big and well known, such as The British Red Cross, Cancer Research UK, and Blind Veterans UK, and newer, smaller specialist charities.

242 In 2012 research from the Charities Aid Foundation showed that throughout her reign she has helped the charities she supports to raise more than £1.4bn.

243 Many children's charities have benefited from The Queen's patronage, including Save the Children, the NSPCC, Action for Children, Royal Navy and Royal Marines Children's Fund, and Barnardo's.

244 The monarch has always been a keen spectator of sports, but it often surprises people to know that The Queen was a patron of the Welsh Rugby Union, Rugby Football Union and Rugby Football League; her sporting patronage also includes the British Cycling Federation and the British Fencing Association.

245 As you would expect, The Queen is patron of many equestrian charities, including The Jockey Club and the National Horseracing Museum.

246 The Sandringham Women's Institute proudly boasts The Queen as its President – and its meetings take place on her land. In 2009 The Queen addressed the club: 'In this time of change and uncertainty I think the WI's traditional values of playing your part through education and public debate are just as important as ever. By helping women to improve their lives and the lives of those around them, the WI is playing a valuable role.'

247 When The Queen was a baby, in 1927, she was given a doll dressed in a Guide uniform as a present from the Guides and Brownies of Ballarat, Australia. Her association with the organisation has never ceased, even after her days as a Girl Guide came to an end. She is patron of the Girl Guide Association, and also of the Sea Cadets, another organisation with which she has personal connections.

248 In 2005 The Queen became the first patron of a new charity about which she felt very strongly. The Holocaust Memorial Day Trust was founded to mark 27 January as a day on which communities all over the world take time to pause and remember the atrocities committed by the Nazis, and to strive to ensure that the world becomes a more tolerant and fair society. When The Queen stepped down as patron after her 90th birthday, she ensured that HRH Prince Charles, took over her role.

249 The Queen has always been passionate about animal welfare and this is reflected in many of the charities that can or did count her as their patron, including the RSPCA, Battersea Dogs' Home, The British Horse Society, The RSPB and Dogs Trust – and even The Royal Pigeon Racing Association. The first royal racing pigeons were given to Queen Victoria by the King of the Belgians. The sport became a popular royal pastime, and one of its keenest adherents was The Queen's father.

250 One of the oldest charities to have The Queen as its patron is also one of the most obscure: the British Open Brass Band Championship. The Open was founded in 1853 in Manchester and has held regular competitions ever since. The Queen became its patron in 2001.

'We haven't laughed so much for years'

The Royal Variety Performance holds a special place in the nation's heart. While many theatrical stars have shone and gone (some instantly forgotten), the show endures. Each annual performance is in aid of The Royal Variety Charity, whose patron is The Queen.

251 In 1947, two weeks before her wedding, Princess Elizabeth attended her first Royal Variety Performance with her fiancé, Philip Mountbatten. The acts that year included the American duo Laurel and Hardy, impressionist Jack Durant, transvestite ventriloquist Bobbie Kimber, and the singer Gracie Fields. King George VI spoke warmly of the evening, saying 'We haven't laughed so much for years' – a poignant comment just two years after the end of the War.

252 Anxious organisers of the 1952 Royal Variety Performance were gratified by the new queen's comment on their programme: 'This is the best show of all'. Stars included The Beverley Sisters, Norman Wisdom and Maurice Chevalier. Naval officer Prince Philip was particularly amused by Tony Hancock's sketch about the Royal Navy. Bud Flanagan began the show by giving a jokey warning to the rest of the audience, 'and don't look up to see if The Queen is laughing first, or you'll get on her blinking nerves'.

253 There wasn't much to laugh about towards the end of 1956. A crisis over the control of the Suez Canal escalated, as Britain and France sided with the Israelis and the Soviet Union backed the Egyptians under Nassar. The Royal Variety Performance was cancelled as the nation coped with the prospect of another war. The crisis was averted in 1957, and the RVP returned in all its splendour.

Opposite page: **(far left) Princess Margaret and The Queen enjoy the performance of 1952. (Left) The Queen meets Marilyn Monroe in 1956.**

This page: **(below left) Pudsey's finest moment, as he meets The Queen after his starring performance in 2012. (Below right) American singer Lady Gaga meets The Queen after the Royal Variety Performance held in Blackpool in 2009.**

The Silver Jubilee
Royal Variety Gala

In the presence of Her Majesty

Queen Elizabeth II

On the evening of Monday 21 November 1977
at The Palladium, London

The Silver Jubilee Royal Variety Gala

Bob Hope
as Host

Julie Andrews
Paul Anka
Pam Ayres
Harry Belafonte
Brotherhood of Man
Tommy Cooper
Alan King
Cleo Laine with John Dankworth and John Williams
Little and Large
Shirley MacLaine
Jim Henson's Muppets
Choreography by Gillian Lynne
Rudolph Nureyev with Yokio Morishipa
and other Guest Stars
Jack Parnell and his Orchestra

Bob Hope appears by courtesy of Texaco
Total production conceived and devised by Garry Smith & Dwight Hemion

254 In the 1968 show, singer Diana Ross paid tribute to the recently murdered civil rights activist Martin Luther King, saying, 'Let our efforts be as determined as those of Dr Martin Luther King, who had a dream that all God's children ... could join hands and sing'. She reminded the audience that in some American states black and white people had to use different doors at a theatre. She received a standing ovation.

255 Although the Royal Variety Performance was cancelled in 1956, that autumn The Queen attended a London premiere, of the film *The Battle of the River Plate*. Also in attendance were Marilyn Monroe and her husband, playwright Arthur Miller. Both The Queen and Monroe had recently celebrated their 30th birthdays and a rare image shows the two women smiling at each other. Despite The Queen's many attendances at film premieres, this was the only time the actress met her, as Monroe died just six years later.

256 Beatle John Lennon made headlines – and history – at the Royal Variety Performance in 1963. The Queen didn't attend – she was pregnant – but the Queen Mother and Princess Margaret saw the Fab Four perform 'Twist and Shout', and to hear Lennon say 'For our last number I'd like to ask your help. Would the people in the cheaper seats clap your hands? And the rest of you, if you'll just rattle your jewellery.' The Queen Mother was reported to have described The Beatles afterwards as 'most intriguing'.

257 In 1967 Sandie Shaw appeared onstage in a highly fashionable mini skirt, but changed her outfit before meeting The Queen. When quizzed about the skirt swap, Ms Shaw commented, 'A mini is fine on stage, but I am told it would be more elegant to be presented to The Queen in something a little more special!'

258 The Royal Variety Performance on 21 November 1977 was a special Gala show for the Silver Jubilee year. Bob Hope performed as solo host; his intended co-host, Bing Crosby, died a few weeks before the show. The Sex Pistols may have been storming up the charts, but The Queen, Prince Philip and Prince Charles were treated to a rather more sedate line-up, including Julie Andrews, Pam Ayres, Rudoph Nureyev and The Muppets.

259 The Royal Variety Performance celebrated its 100th year in 2012, moving venue from the London Palladium to the Albert Hall. The enormous list of human stars was overshadowed by the canine star of the show: Pudsey the dancing dog, joint winner of *Britain's Got Talent* (together with his owner, Ashleigh).

260 In 2017 The Queen's grandson Prince William found himself taking part, unexpectedly. Much to the amusement of the Duchess of Cambridge, the show's host, Miranda Hart, persuaded the Prince to call out her catchphrase 'such fun' whenever she gave the signal.

Elizabeth the inspiring

Music, poetry and new dishes have been created in honour of The Queen. Even the costume designer of *Star Wars* mentions her as a muse for one of his characters!

261 Probably the most famous dish created for Elizabeth II is the one created for her coronation banquet in 1953. Looking for a special dish, florist and author Constance Spry came up with a recipe for cold chicken in a curried cream sauce, served with a salad of herbed rice and green peas. Coronation Chicken has been enjoyed ever since.

262 In honour of the young Princess Elizabeth and the new baby Princess Margaret Rose, Sir Edward Elgar composed *Nursery Suite*, in 1930. At this date Elgar was 'Master of the King's Musick' for King George V, the princesses' grandfather. *Nursery Suite* was one of his last compositions, although within it he incorporated elements of his earliest works, written in his youth.

263 Benjamin Britten's opera *Gloriana* was commissioned for the coronation. The newly crowned queen attended its premiere, at London's Royal Opera House, on 8 June 1953. The opera is based on Victorian author Lytton Strachey's book *Elizabeth and Essex*, about Queen Elizabeth I. *Gloriana* was performed at the Royal Opera House again in June 2013, to mark the 60th anniversary of the coronation.

264 When US President Dwight Eisenhower visited The Queen at Balmoral in 1960, he was served homemade drop scones, which he liked so much he asked for the recipe. Buckingham Palace sent details of what have become known as The Queen's Drop Scones, shared far and wide. Check out the recipe online!

265 Sir John Betjeman was knighted by The Queen in 1969, three years before being made Poet Laureate (he died in post in 1984). For the Silver Jubilee in 1977 Betjeman composed his 'Jubilee Hymn', which began, 'In days of

disillusion, However low we've been, To fire us and inspire us, God gave to us our Queen.'

266 In 2007, for The Queen and Prince Philip's 60th wedding anniversary, then-Poet Laureate Andrew Motion wrote the poem *Diamond Wedding*, which included the lines:

*Love found a voice and spoke two names
aloud two private names aloud
two private names,
though breezed through public air
and joined them in a life where duty spoke
in languages their tenderness could share*

267 *Sing* was composed by Gary Barlow and Andrew Lloyd-Webber and performed by musicians from across the Commonwealth for The Queen's Diamond Jubilee. More than 200 performers took part – including Prince Harry, who made a surprise appearance playing the tambourine. Barlow wrote the lyrics at Treetops in Kenya, the place where Princess Elizabeth learnt of the death of her father and was told she was now queen.

268 Nadiya Hussain, winner of the TV show *Great British Bake-Off*, was thrilled to be commissioned to create a cake for The Queen's 90th birthday. The cake was a three-tiered orange drizzle cake, decorated in luxurious purple and gold icing.

269 Carol Ann Duffy, the Poet Laureate, in 2013 composed her poem *The Crown* for the 60th anniversary of the coronation. Its final lines echo The Queen's own words:

Its jewels glow, virtues; loyalty's ruby, blood-deep; sapphire's ice resilience; emerald evergreen; the shy pearl, humility. My whole life, whether it be long or short, devoted to your service. Not lightly worn.

270 When Hollywood costume designer Michael Kaplan was working on Carrie Fisher's clothes for her role as General Leia in *Star Wars: The Last Jedi* he modelled her look on that of The Queen. He was particularly inspired by Pietro Annigoni's 1969 portrait, *Her Majesty in Robes of the British Empire* (see page 144). Kaplan said of Leia's character: 'I wanted her to look as beautiful and regal as possible.'

St Paul's Cathedral
in London was the
magnificent setting
for a Service of
Thanksgiving for the
Queen's 90th birthday
in June 2016.

ELIZABETH'S WORLD

The Queen's reign has been marked by radical change, with revolutions in science, technology, medicine and space travel occurring at an unprecedented speed and scale. The Queen has embraced many of these advances; she was the first monarch to fly on a supersonic aircraft, and is the first British monarch to send a Tweet! She has lent her name to projects working to protect the planet and transformed her Royal Family, helping to create a new generation of outgoing, emotionally expressive and popular young royals. She has grieved with us following disasters and atrocities, and witnessed with us the rise of punk, the fall of the Berlin Wall and the birth of the first test tube baby.

As possibly the most photographed woman on the planet, The Queen has enjoyed looking back out through a lens and recording the rapidly changing world around her. Here she is in the 1950s, just before she became Queen, pursuing one of her favourite hobbies (see also page 38).

Ten 20th-century Prime Ministers

Over her long reign The Queen has seen many Prime Ministers come and go – she must have enjoyed telling Tony Blair (Prime Minister 1997–2007) that he wasn't even born when she was crowned!

271 Every week The Queen holds a meeting with her Prime Minister. As a constitutional monarch, The Queen is politically neutral, but she can offer advice and has the right to express her views. After a general election the newly elected leader has a meeting with The Queen to 'request permission to form a government', and a Prime Minister must also request a meeting with The Queen if they wish to resign.

272 Although **Sir Winston Churchill** lost the election directly after the War in 1945, by 1951 he was back in office, making him The Queen's first Prime Minister. When he suffered a stroke, shortly after her coronation, he kept it a secret from his cabinet, but he confided in The Queen. In a letter to her written in 1955 Churchill described her as 'a sparkling presence'.

273 Conservative MP **Anthony Eden** became Prime Minister in 1955, when Winston Churchill retired. Initially The Queen and her new minister had an easy relationship and were said to talk freely,

but she disapproved of his handling of the Suez Crisis – the event that led to his resignation after only two years in office.

274 **Harold Macmillan** replaced Anthony Eden in 1957, at the head of a divided Conservative cabinet. He remained in office for six years and kept meticulous diaries. He wrote of The Queen: 'She showed, as her father used to, an uncanny knowledge of details and personalities. She must read the telegrams very carefully.'

275 When the Earl of Home renounced his peerage so that he could become Prime Minister in 1963, he became known simply as **Alec Douglas-Home**. Queen Elizabeth The Queen Mother and he had been childhood friends, so The Queen already knew him well. It was speculated that the talk at their weekly meetings was more likely to have been about horses and dogs than politics.

276 In 1964 **Harold Wilson** became the first Labour Prime Minister

Opposite page: (left) The Queen and her eldest children with Prime Minster Sir Winston Churchill in 1954. *Main image:* Five of the Queen's Prime Ministers (left to right) Tony Blair, Margaret Thatcher, Sir Edward Heath, James Callaghan and John Major, gathered in 2002 to celebrate the start of her Golden Jubilee celebrations. *This page:* (bottom) The Queen with Sir Harold Wilson in June 1969. (Below) The Queen greets Anthony Eden in 1956.

of The Queen's reign, after 13 years of Conservative rule. He and The Queen enjoyed a harmonious relationship. Wilson found the world of politics gruelling and wrote of his relief at knowing that The Queen would keep whatever he said confidential and not leak it to the papers. Barbara Castle commented that Wilson allowed The Queen to 'feel at ease'.

277 After Wilson's sudden resignation in 1976, **James Callaghan** became Prime Minister for three years. He and The Queen got on well, and The Queen liked the fact that her new Prime Minister had been in the Royal Navy, although Callaghan wrote that their relationship was a case of 'friendliness but not friendship'.

278 It was expected that The Queen and Britain's first female Prime Minister, **Margaret Thatcher** (1979–90), would have an easy relationship, especially as they were the same age, but the media soon became convinced that was not the case. Official files, declassified in 2017, state that The Queen was angry with

Thatcher in 1987 after she refused to join 47 other Commonwealth leaders in backing tighter sanctions against South Africa, in an attempt to bring about an end to apartheid.

279 **John Major**, Prime Minister from 1990 to 1997, wrote of his monarch: 'One can say to The Queen absolutely anything. Even thoughts you perhaps don't want to share with your Cabinet at a particular time you can say to The Queen, and I did.'

280 In 1997 the Labour party and its leader **Tony Blair** won a landslide election victory. The Queen pointed out to him that when she came to the throne, he was not yet born! Following Princess Diana's tragic death that year, the Royal Family went through its lowest period. Tony Blair helped The Queen manage public opinion, famously delivering his popular 'people's princess' speech. In an interview in 2010, Blair said he had advised The Queen and that he had felt a duty 'to protect the monarchy from itself'.

Ten memorable events

Among the world-class occasions of The Queen's long reign, there are certain 'moments' that stand out in the memories of her British subjects.

281 On 6 May 1954, 25-year-old Roger Bannister, a medical student at St Mary's Hospital, London, was preparing to race against the University of Oxford. Having already worked a hospital shift, Bannister took a train to Oxford and raced around the track, becoming the first person to run a mile in under four minutes. His recorded time was 3 minutes 59.4 seconds. In 1975 Bannister – by now a respected neurologist – was knighted by The Queen.

282 Elvis fever first hit the UK when his single *Heartbreak Hotel* reached No. 2 in the UK Charts on 12 May 1956. British teenagers swooned over the 'dangerous' US hip-wiggler, and within a couple of years Presley's popularity had started to eclipse that of home-grown talent, including Cliff Richard and Tommy Steele.

283 By the mid-1960s Britain was firmly in love with the motor car, but far too many deaths were occurring on its roads. In January 1966 a new Road Safety Bill was introduced, which set a new limit for how much alcohol a driver could consume. In 1967 the police began using the newly created breathalyser, to test whether drivers had broken the law. This dramatically reduced the number of deaths caused by drunken driving.

284 On 1 July 1967 the BBC made its first colour television broadcast live from Centre Court. Wimbledon was shown on BBC Two, and the channel's controller, David Attenborough, announced that at least five hours per week would now be in colour. By the end of the year, 80 per cent of the BBC's television programmes were in colour.

Opposite page: **Roger Bannister becomes the first man to officially run a mile in under four minutes on 6 May 1954.**

This page: **(left to right) Pre-Decimal-day poster to prepare the public** in February 1971; **Edwin 'Buzz' Aldrin on the moon, photographed by fellow astronaut Neil Armstrong on 20 July 1969; Red Rum wins the Grand National for the third time on 2 April 1977.**

285 On 20 July 1969 astronaut Neil Armstrong became the first person to walk on the moon. He was part of the *Apollo II* mission, together with Edwin 'Buzz' Aldrin and Michael Collins. All over Britain, people crowded around television sets to watch the historic moment being broadcast.

286 On 14 February 1971 Britain finally embraced decimalisation. Some Britons found it easier than others to move on from old 'ten bob notes' (50p) and tanners (2½p). The 'piffling' decimal halfpenny coin annoyed everyone, until the remaining coins that hadn't been lost down the backs of sofas or been eaten by washing machines were finally withdrawn in 1984.

287 At midnight, as the year 1972 changed into 1973, a Union Jack was raised in Brussels, at the headquarters of the EEC, or the European Economic Community. Prime Minister Ted Heath, said in his speech, '[In] our

everyday lives we will find there is a great cross-fertilisation of knowledge and information, not only in business but in every other sphere. And this will enable us to be more efficient and more competitive in gaining more markets not only in Europe but in the rest of the world.'

288 In the year of The Queen's Silver Jubilee, a large number of

newspaper headlines were devoted to one very special horse. On 2 April 1977 the much-loved Red Rum won the Grand National for a record third time. His trainer, Ginger McCain, was quoted as saying 'All I wanted to do was cry'.

289 When London hosted the Olympics and Paralympics in 2012, a brand new Olympic park and village were created in East London. The Paralympics were the most successful ever, selling more tickets, raising more money and being broadcast to more people around the world than ever before. Thus 2012 ushered in a new age of Paralympic sport.

290 On 6 February 2012 The Queen became the second British monarch in history to celebrate a Diamond Jubilee and the whole country became involved in celebrating her reign. Thousands of events took place around Britain and millions of people took part – such as the 8.5 million people who joined in the Big Jubilee Lunches, despite torrential rain. One highlight of the celebrations was The Thames Pageant, on 3 June, in which 1,000 boats from all over the world participated.

ELIZABETH'S WORLD

Ten 'firsts' for The Queen

Elizabeth II has reigned over an era when technological and medical advances have been phenomenal, and in which British society has undergone many crucial changes. She has experienced many 'firsts', most of which she has appeared to enjoy!

291 The Queen was the first female member of the Royal Family to serve in the armed forces: in 1942, as Princess Elizabeth, she was made Colonel of the Grenadier Guards. After her 18th birthday, in 1945, she joined the Auxiliary Territorial Service, known as the ATS, as a second subaltern. She learnt to strip and repair engines, and how to drive a car, a truck and an ambulance.

292 In April 1955 The Queen became the first sovereign to enter 10 Downing Street. She broke with tradition to attend Sir Winston Churchill's farewell party – the former Prime Minister was retiring at the age of 80.

293 In 1966 The Queen and the Duke of Edinburgh were among the 97,000-strong crowd watching the football World Cup at Wembley Stadium. Following England's 4–2 win over West Germany, The Queen became the first monarch to present the England football squad with the coveted trophy. She handed it to a beaming Bobby Moore, team captain.

Opposite: **The Queen sends her first royal Tweet under her own name in October 2014: 'It is a pleasure to open the Information Age exhibition today at @ScienceMuseum and I hope people will enjoy visiting. Elizabeth R.'**

Above: **A slightly strained breakfast as cameras intrude for the first time during filming of *Royal Family* in 1969.**
Left: **The Queen presents the Jules Rimet Trophy to captain Bobby Moore after England's 4–2 victory over West Germany in the football World Cup of 1966.**

294 The Queen was the first monarch to permit a documentary to be made about their family, and possibly the first to regret it. For a year the royals were followed by a camera crew, who were allowed unprecedented access to intimate family moments. The 90-minute film, *Royal Family*, was broadcast by the BBC in June 1969, and then shown on ITV. The film was considered so intrusive that it has not been shown since.

295 The Queen is the first reigning monarch to travel by London Underground. She took the inaugural ride on the Victoria Line from Green Park on 7 March 1969. Archive film of the day also shows her taking the controls of the train at Green Park, the stop nearest Buckingham Palace!

296 The Queen is the first British monarch to circle the globe by aeroplane. She is also the first monarch to fly on a supersonic aircraft – she flew on Concorde in 1977. The Queen is the only person in Britain not to require a passport, as all passports are issued in her name. She is, however, required to undertake an identity check at all borders.

297 In October 1986 The Queen became the first British monarch to visit mainland China. Deng Xiaoping was in charge at the time, and Britain and China were locked in discussion about the future of Hong Kong. The Queen and Prince Philip spent a week in China, visiting the Great Wall and the Terracotta Warriors.

298 In 2012 The Queen became the first monarch to be filmed in 3D, when Sky News captured her Christmas speech in three dimensions. She was photographed laughing while wearing 3D glasses to watch herself on screen. The glasses were adorned with a Q in Swarovski crystals; she had previously worn them on a visit to Toronto, Canada, in 2010.

299 While opening the Information Age exhibition at London's Science Museum in 2014, The Queen became the first British monarch to tweet! She posted on the @BritishMonarchy account 'It is a pleasure to open the Information Age exhibition today at @ScienceMuseum and I hope people will enjoy visiting. Elizabeth R'.

300 In 2017 The Queen became the first British monarch to reach a Sapphire Jubilee, after reigning for a record 65 years. The Royal Mint marked the occasion with a range of commemorative coins, and Royal Mail issued a £5 stamp in brilliant sapphire blue.

Opposite page: **(top) The Queen, meets performers in the Great Hall of the People after a banquet during her historic first visit to China in 1986. (Bottom) The Queen's Christmas speech to the Commonwealth is broadcast for the first time in 3D in 2012.**

This page: **The Queen takes her first Underground ride as a reigning monarch to celebrate the opening of the Victoria Line on 7 March 1969.**

Significant royal tours

The Queen has visited over 120 countries, often insisting on travelling to regions her government considered too dangerous. The one country The Queen refused to visit, however, was apartheid-controlled South Africa, until apartheid had ended.

301 The Royal Tour of 1953–4 saw The Queen become the first reigning British monarch to visit **Australia**, **New Zealand** and **Fiji**. The new queen and her husband travelled over 50,000 miles and visited 14 countries. It was claimed the royal luggage weighed around 12 tons and that it included more than 200 pairs of white gloves!

302 The royal yacht reached Australia on 3 February 1954, mooring in Sydney. During their sometimes gruelling two months in Australia, the royal couple covered more than 10,000 miles, largely by aeroplane. When they visited Melbourne, around 70,000 ex-servicemen and women crowded into the Melbourne Cricket Ground (the MCG) to see The Queen.

303 Official estimates of the time claimed that three-quarters of the Australian population and three-quarters of the New Zealand population saw the royal couple during their tour. New Zealanders recalled that previously unsealed roads were sealed so the royal cars could drive on them, and many remembered seeing sheep with their coats dyed red, white and blue to celebrate The Queen's visit.

304 The Queen and the Duke of Edinburgh visited **Ghana** in 1961, four years after the country had gained independence. While the tour was being prepared, stories of bombings in Ghana hit the British headlines. Politicians questioned whether the visit was advisable. The Queen, however, was resolute, famously telling Prime Minister Harold Macmillan: 'I am not a film star,

I am the head of the Commonwealth and I am paid to face any risks.' In Ghana, tens of thousands of people lined the streets to see the royal couple.

305 The Queen made her first visit to **Canada** in 1951, when she was still Princess Elizabeth, and it has become one of her favourite places. On her first visit as Queen, in 1957, she won hearts by giving speeches in English and French, and by attending a state dinner in a gown decorated with green velvet maple leaves.

306 In 1959 The Queen and the Duke of Edinburgh made history by undertaking the longest royal tour in Canadian history: they spent 45 days in the country, during which time they travelled to all ten provinces and covered over 15,000 miles. The Queen returned to Canada in 2010 for her 22nd official visit!

Left: **The Queen and President Kwame Nkrumah during her visit to Ghana in 1961.**

Above: **The Royal Tour of 1953–4 was celebrated in many souvenir magazine issues.**

This page: **(above) The Queen receives a bouquet from a child in Fiji during her royal tour of the Pacific in 1954. (Below) Surf lifesavers march up to The Queen's dais during the Surf Carnival staged in her honour at Sydney's Bondi Beach, February 1954.**

307 On 12 February 1979 The Queen and Prince Philip flew on Concorde to the Gulf state of **Kuwait**, marking the country's first visit from a British sovereign. They had been invited by the Amir of Kuwait, HH Sheikh Jaber Al-Ahmed Al-Sabah, who greeted them as they stepped off the plane. The royal couple spent three weeks in the Middle East, also visiting Bahrain, Saudi Arabia, Qatar, the United Arab Emirates and Oman.

308 The Queen was the first British monarch to visit **India** after the country gained independence from British rule. She and the Duke of Edinburgh visited for the first time in 1961 and have returned twice, in 1983 and in 1997. Each of the visits has been fraught with political difficulties, especially her third visit, which was her first public engagement since the death of Princess Diana.

309 The 1997 tour of India included a visit by The Queen to Jallianwala Bagh, the site of an infamous massacre by British troops in 1919. The Queen gave an apology, but many Indian activists thought her words inadequate.

310 Very few tourists have been lucky enough to visit the tiny **South Pacific** island nation of Nauru – but The Queen has! The 1982 royal tour of the South Pacific also saw The Queen and Prince Philip visit Tuvalu, Kiribati, the Solomon Islands, Fiji, and Papua New Guinea, as well as Australia.

Ten royal residences

The Queen and her family enjoy the use of a variety of homes over the UK. Some are royal palaces, owned by the Crown and held in trust by the monarch, others are privately owned.

311 Princess Elizabeth was born at **17 Bruton Street**, in London's fashionable Mayfair. It was the home of her maternal grandparents, the Earl and Countess of Strathmore and Kinghorne. Sadly, the house was demolished in the 1930s. There are two commemorative plaques on the site of the building: one for her Silver Jubilee and one for her Diamond Jubilee.

312 In 1927, when Princess Elizabeth's parents returned from their royal tour, the family moved into **145 Piccadilly**, near several of London's parks, where baby Elizabeth was frequently taken out in her pram by the nanny. The house had 25 bedrooms, a ballroom and a lift. At the start of the Second World War the house was used as a charity office; sadly, it was destroyed by bombs.

313 The new King George VI, Queen Elizabeth, Princess Elizabeth and Princess Margaret Rose moved into **Buckingham Palace** two months after Edward VIII's abdication in 1936. The palace has been the monarch's official London residence since 1837. It has 775 rooms, including 52 royal and guest bedrooms and 92 offices.

314 During the Second World War the princesses were sent away from London to live at **Royal Lodge** in Windsor – its walls, which had formerly been painted a pale pink, were now painted green, as a form of camouflage. Later in the war the princesses spent much of their time at **Windsor Castle**, where both they and the Crown Jewels (as it was revealed in 2017) were to be kept safe. The jewels were wrapped up in paper and placed in an underground vault.

315 The first members of the Royal Family to visit **Balmoral** were Queen Victoria and Prince Albert, who bought the old castle in 1852 – and promptly set about building a new one just a year later. In the 1930s King George VI and Queen Elizabeth began visiting, and grew very fond of the castle. Today Balmoral owes much to the hard work of the Duke of Edinburgh, who took on an active role in managing the estate and its gardens. The Queen and her family spend much of the summer at Balmoral.

316 Beautiful Sandringham Castle, in Norfolk, has been home to the British Royal Family since 1862. The estate encompasses over 20,000 acres of land and employs more than 200 people. In 1977, during The Queen's Silver Jubilee, the castle was opened to the public for the first time.

317 Clarence House is a legacy of the great John Nash (1752–1835), the architect responsible for creating many of London's most important Regency buildings. In 1947 the house became home to Princess Elizabeth and her new husband, the Duke of Edinburgh. The Queen Mother moved into Clarence House in 1953 and became its longest-serving resident, living there very happily until her death in 2002.

318 The Palace of Holyroodhouse in Edinburgh, the Queen's official residence in Scotland, is most frequently in the news during Holyrood Week, a series of royal events and parties that take place at the end of June and beginning of July. The location of the

Opposite page: **The magnificent baroque East Front of Hampton Court Palace, owned by The Queen in right of Crown.**

Top: **Sandringham Castle in Norfolk.**
Above: **The graceful Georgian exterior of Hillsborough Castle, The Queen's official residence in Northern Ireland.**

palace has an impressively long history, dating back to its origins as an Augustinian monastery in the 12th century.

319 Hillsborough Castle, a splendid late Georgian manor house in Northern Ireland, has been the official residence of the Royal Family since 1921. Since 1970 the castle has been the residence of the Secretary of State for Northern Ireland and it continues to be the official royal residence of Her Majesty The Queen. In 2009 The Queen met Mary Macaleese, then President of Ireland, for the first time on Irish soil. Since April 2014 Hillsborough Castle has been managed by Historic Royal Palaces.

320 While not strictly 'residences', The Queen owns some iconic and beautiful royal buildings in right of Crown in England. Among these heritage sites are the Tower of London, Hampton Court Palace, Kensington Palace, the Banqueting House in Whitehall and Kew Palace, all open to the public and managed by Historic Royal Palaces.

Ten world leaders who have met The Queen

The Queen has been horse-riding with one American president, been described as 'Truly my favourite person' by another, and was on first name terms with Nelson Mandela. Not all her meetings with world leaders have been so cordial, however.

321 The Queen first met Emperor Haile Selassie I when he visited London in 1954. In February 1965 The Queen and the Duke of Edinburgh made a state visit to Ethiopia, where they were welcomed at the airport by the Emperor and were given a state dinner at the Emperor's 'old palace' – in the gardens of which were kept his pet lions.

322 President Charles de Gaulle and his wife Yvonne visited Britain in 1960, shortly after the birth of Prince Andrew. The visit was deemed a great success, with French newspapers describing it as 'fantastic' and 'unforgettable'.

323 When the King and Queen of Nepal visited Britain in 1960

The Queen and Princess Margaret were amongst the crowds waiting to meet their special train at Victoria Station, which, in very British style, was delayed by fog.

324 On a state visit to Italy in May 1961 The Queen and the Duke of Edinburgh were granted a private meeting with the Pope, which lasted for 25 minutes. Pope John XXIII had been elected in 1958 and remained in office for less than five years, dying of cancer in 1963.

325 In the early summer of 1961, President John F Kennedy and his wife, Jackie, visited Britain on a private holiday. The Queen gave a dinner party at Buckingham Palace in their honour, on 5 June, to which the President brought a

small gift for The Queen: a signed photograph of himself, presented in a silver frame from Tiffany & Co. A state visit was being planned when Kennedy was assassinated in 1963.

326 In 1971 Emperor Hirohito and Empress Kojun of Japan made a controversial official visit to Britain. The memories of the war were still raw, and the *New York Times* noted that the crowds in London were 'unusually quiet'. At an official dinner The Queen addressed the issue: 'We cannot pretend that the relations between our two peoples have always been peaceful and friendly. However, it is precisely this experience which should make us all the more determined never to let it happen again.'

From left: **US President John F Kennedy and the First Lady, Jacqueline, with The Queen and Prince Philip at a dinner held in their honour in 1961; The Queen with Japanese Emperor Hirohito and his wife, Nagako, during their state visit in 1971; The Queen and Nelson Mandela during his visit to London in 2013: she had previously met him in South Africa shortly after his release from prison in 1995.**

327 US President Ronald Reagan and his wife Nancy stayed at Windsor Castle in 1982. During the state visit, the newspapers were full of images of the monarch and the president riding in Windsor Great Park.

328 In 1995 The Queen was welcomed to South Africa by new President Nelson Mandela, just five years out of prison. Mandela's personal assistant, Zelda la Grange, wrote in her memoirs: 'I was struck by the warm friendship between Madiba and The Queen. "Oh Elizabeth," he would say when he greeted her, and she would respond: "Hello, Nelson." I think he was one of the very few people who called her by her first name and she seemed to be amused by it.'

Left: **Barack and Michelle Obama drop in for lunch at Windsor in April 2016. They met The Queen for the first time in 2009.** *Below left:* **The Queen in 2013 with the President of South Korea, Park Geun-hye, during a state visit.**

Below right: **The Queen and Emperor of Ethiopia, Haile Selassie, in 1954.** *Below:* **US President Ronald Reagan riding Centennial with the Queen on her horse, Burmese, in the grounds of Windsor Castle in 1982.**

329 In 2013 The Queen met South Korea's first female president, Park Geun-hye. She was invited to stay at Buckingham Palace and her visit was celebrated by a 41-gun salute in Hyde Park, by the King's Troop Royal Horse Artillery.

330 The Queen met US President Barack Obama and his wife, Michelle, for the first time in 2009, and in 2011 the Obamas were invited to Buckingham Palace. In 2016 the presidential couple visited The Queen and her family at Windsor Castle for a private lunch. At a press conference during his state visit in 2011 President Obama said of The Queen: 'She is truly one of my favourite people.'

ELIZABETH'S WORLD

Ten terrifying moments

The Queen's reign has not been without some frightening and potentially disastrous moments for the monarch herself, including kidnap and assassination attempts.

331 In 1966 a block of concrete and a bottle were thrown at the car in which The Queen and Duke of Edinburgh were travelling on a visit to Belfast, Northern Ireland. The concrete block damaged the car bonnet but did not injure anyone. The Queen and the Duke were sheltered by a plastic shield erected over the top of the car.

332 In 1974 an audacious attempt was made to kidnap the recently married Princess Anne. A gunman named Ian Ball blocked the Princess's car and shot her bodyguard, a young policeman and a journalist – luckily none of the three was killed. A passing motorist, a former boxer, Ronald Russell, punched Ball and helped police to capture him. Russell was awarded the George Cross by The Queen, who also thanked him personally 'as a mother'.

333 In the middle of the night, on 9 July 1982, The Queen awoke to discover a strange man in her bedroom. The intruder, Michael Fagan, admitted that it was the second time he had broken in to Buckingham Palace in a month. The Queen managed to alert footman Paul Whybrew, who distracted Fagan by offering him a drink. After being arrested, Fagan was sent for psychiatric evaluation.

334 Early on Easter Monday 1986, fire broke out at Hampton Court Palace, probably started by a candle in the bedroom of 86-year-old grace-and-favour resident Lady Daphne Gale. Lady Gale sadly perished and the blaze destroyed much of the King's State Apartments. The Queen, visibly upset, came to see the damage later that day. Restoration was completed in July 1992; in November that year a fire destroyed 155 rooms at Windsor Castle. It began in Queen Victoria's Private Chapel, when a faulty spotlight ignited a curtain. Five years of painstaking restoration was completed in time for The Queen's 50th wedding anniversary.

335 In June 1981, while riding along The Mall to the Trooping of the Colour, The Queen was shot at by 17-year-old Marcus Serjeant. He fired six rounds of blanks, before being disarmed by a member of the Scots Guard. The crowd panicked, but The Queen seemed imperturbable as she kept her seat and calmly soothed her frightened horse.

336 When war broke out in 1982 between Britain and Argentina over the Falkland Islands, Prince Andrew was serving in the Navy. When his ship was deployed, the government wanted to move him to a safe desk job, but the

Main image: **The devastating fire at Windsor Castle in 1992, which destroyed over 155 rooms.**

Above: **Stained glass window in the Private Chapel, commemorating the heroic firefighters who tackled the blaze.**

Prince refused and The Queen backed her son's decision, despite the danger.

337 The pessimistic might have predicted this, but during The Queen's 13th visit to Australia in 2000 a man was arrested trying to approach her as she arrived at the Opera House. He was found to be carrying a home-made bomb and a knife.

338 Prince Harry served in the army for ten years, including two tours of war-torn Afghanistan. In 2009 the breaking of a media embargo revealed his location, putting the Prince and his entire regiment in increased danger. Although he had to be recalled home, the Prince returned to Afghanistan in 2012, with – he told the media – his grandmother's blessing.

339 The number of celebrity deaths in 2016 started a superstitious belief that the year was cursed. A fake BBC Twitter account tweeted that The Queen had died in 'unknown' circumstances, and the story gained momentum because she had been too unwell to attend church on Christmas Day. Conspiracy theorists claimed that the mainstream media was covering up the truth, until Buckingham Palace issued a press release to explain that The Queen and Duke of Edinburgh 'continue to recover from their heavy colds'.

340 In 2017 papers were released claiming that The Queen had been targeted by a would-be teenage assassin when she visited New Zealand in 1981. A former police officer admitted that 17-year-old Christopher John Lewis had fired a gun, fortunately without injuring anyone. Lewis was later imprisoned for the murder of a young woman and the kidnap of her child; he committed suicide in prison.

Royal trains, boats and planes

The Queen has used many splendid vehicles during her reign, some more comfortable than others. The fabulous Gold State Coach looks much more impressive than it feels, whereas the Royal Yacht *Britannia* had a very special place in The Queen's affections.

341 The golden state coach was created for King George III in 1762. It was designed by William Chambers and created by master coachmaker Samuel Butler. The coach is only used for very special occasions, but despite its beauty and history, The Queen revealed in a documentary that riding in it is extremely uncomfortable and it is certainly *not* her favourite mode of transport!

342 The Royal Yacht *Britannia* was commissioned by King George VI and launched by The Queen in Scotland in 1953. *Britannia* even had a garage for the royal Rolls-Royce! Many heads of state were invited to dine on board *Britannia*, including Sir Winston Churchill, Bill Clinton and Nelson Mandela. The Queen bade an emotional farewell to her much-loved yacht on 11 December 1997.

343 The concept of a dedicated royal train was introduced for Queen Victoria. Although the modern royals have used trains throughout The Queen's reign, it was decided to create a special royal train for The Queen's Silver Jubilee tour in 1977. The Royal Train is decorated in claret-coloured livery and comprises sleeping cars, dining cars and lounge carriages.

344 However, The Queen doesn't use a special train for 'normal' travel, which often surprises Norfolk commuters. Many have been amazed to spot The Queen sipping tea in a first class carriage on their Great Northern train, returning to London from a Christmas at Sandringham.

345 Concorde, the world's first supersonic aircraft, was a joint French and British project. The Queen travelled on Concorde for the first time in 1977. Aircraft in the fleet were able to fly at a height of 60,000 ft – more than 11 miles above the Earth – and had a cruising speed of 1,350 mph. The last commercial Concorde flight travelled from New York to London on 24 October 2003.

Below: **Princesses Margaret (left) and Elizabeth on the footplate of a steam engine that towed the royal train across South Africa in 1947.**

Bottom: **The Gold State Coach.**

346 In 1969 The Queen declared open the new Victoria Line, part of the London Underground – or 'Tube' – network. She was also filmed taking the controls of a Tube train (see page 95). This was not The Queen's first experience of being on the Tube: in 1939 she and Princess Margaret travelled on the Tube with their governess, 'Crawfie'.

347 For air travel the Royal Family relies on the 32nd Squadron. The fleet at their disposal includes two AW109 helicopters, six BAE-125 and four BAE-146 aeroplanes. The Queen also has her own personal helicopter. On occasion the RAF also provides transport for the Royal Family.

348 The Bentley motor company created the State Limousine for The Queen's Golden Jubilee in 2002. The Queen owns two of the cars and they are decorated with her personal mascot of St George slaying the dragon. In 2009 both

cars – which have a top speed of 130 mph – were converted to use biofuel.

349 In honour of the 2012 Diamond Jubilee, Lord Sterling commissioned a golden barge, *Gloriana*, inspired by images of 18th-century ceremonial Thames barges. *Gloriana* is 88 ft long and 11 ft wide, and powered by 18 oars, as well as two electric inboard engines. She is decorated with The Queen's crests and the Royal Cipher, and is fully wheelchair accessible.

350 In October 1982, on her tour of the South Pacific, The Queen arrived at the tiny nine-island nation of Tuvalu, then a special member of the Commonwealth and home to fewer than 10,000 people. The Queen was provided with transport in the form of a war canoe, in which she was carried aloft. Prince Philip, resplendent in his naval uniform, was carried in another canoe.

The World's most exclusive club

The number of monarchies around the world is steadily dwindling, but The Queen has become a popular figure and is now the world's longest-reigning monarch.

351 Until his death in 2016 **King Bhumibol Adulyadej** of Thailand was the world's longest-reigning monarch. He came to the throne in 1946 aged 18. The King and his wife, Queen Sirikit, made an official visit to Britain in 1960.

352 The King of Sweden, **Carl Gustav XVI**, inherited his throne from his grandfather in 1973. His father, the heir to the throne, had died in a plane crash when Carl was a baby. During his reign the laws of royal succession have been changed to ensure that the oldest child can inherit the throne, regardless of gender. His heir is his daughter, Princess Victoria.

353 **Queen Margrethe II** of Denmark is one of The Queen's good friends, as well as a cousin. In an interview ahead of The Queen's 90th birthday, Queen Margrethe commented of her friend: 'It's her sense of humour that keeps her looking so very good, that keeps her wonderful, in fact.'

354 The royal family of Belgium is headed by **King Philippe** and **Queen Mathilde**. Before succeeding his father to the throne, King Philippe was a fighter pilot in the Belgian Air Force. Before her marriage Queen Mathilde worked as a speech therapist; now she works with a large number of charities.

355 **Hassanal Bolkiah**, Sultan of Brunei, came to the throne in 1967 and is the world's second longest-reigning monarch, after The Queen. The Sultan is also Brunei's Prime Minister, military leader and a general in the police force. He lives in the world's biggest palace, Istana Nurul Iman, and has several residences in London.

356 **King Abdullah II** of Jordan has ruled since 1999, succeeding to the throne a week after his 27th birthday. He was the eldest son of King Hussein

This page: **(top) King Bhumibol and Queen Sirikit of Thailand in 1960. (Above) Queen Margrethe of Denmark in 2000.**

Opposite page: **(top) King Siaosi (George) Tupou V of Tonga is crowned in 2008. (Below left) King Felipe of Spain in July 2017. (Below right) King Mswati III of eSwatini in 1998.**

and Princess Muna Al Hussein. King Abdullah II was educated in England and the USA, including joining the Royal Military Academy at Sandhurst. In 1993 he married Queen Rania, with whom he has two daughters and two sons.

357 **King George Tupou V** of Tonga inherited the throne in 2012 after the death of his brother, who had no legitimate children. Tupou went to school and university in Britain and to university in Australia.

358 **King Felipe VI** became King of Spain in 2014, following the abdication of his father, King Juan Carlos. His wife, Queen Letizia, was a TV news journalist before her marriage. They have two daughters: Leonor, Princess of Asturias (the heir to the throne) and the Infanta Sofía. When Felipe was 8 years old, the Spanish dictator General Franco died and Felipe's father was pronounced King – the first Spanish monarch since 1931.

359 **HSH Prince Albert II** is the monarch of the principality of Monaco. He is the son of Prince Rainier III and Princess Grace – formerly known as the Hollywood star Grace Kelly. The Prince has competed in five Olympic Games, and in 2001 he married a fellow Olympian, South African swimmer and gold medallist Princess Charlene (née Wittstock) – the date of their wedding had to be changed to avoid a clash with an International Olympic Committee meeting!

360 **King Mswati III** of eSwatini (formerly Swaziland) is the last remaining absolute monarch in Sub-Saharan Africa. He was born in 1968, just four months before Swaziland celebrated its independence from Britain. The King was the second child of King Sobhuza II – who had 67 children. In 2017 King Mswati III married his 14th wife.

Media meltdowns

Over the decades the media have become less respectful of privacy or status. The Royal Family have not always had the easiest relationship with the press, and several family members have fallen foul of the Fourth Estate.

361 In 1963 a senior police officer from Adelaide, Australia, broke with the rosy image of a royal tour when he criticised the Australian public for their behaviour in front of The Queen. His controversial comments, reported in *The Melbourne Age*, described thousands of invited guests at a royal garden party as 'a pack of mad dogs'.

362 Prince Philip's robust sense of humour, honed in the Navy, has got him into trouble over the years, and provided much media fodder on slow news days. In one of his more repeatable comments, from 1965, he asked a Scottish driving instructor, 'How do you keep the natives off the booze long enough to get them through the test?'

363 In 1960, 30 members of the Welsh Nationalist Party turned down their invitations to a royal garden party, hosted in Cardiff by The Queen and Prince Philip and arranged by the Minister for Welsh Affairs, Henry Brooke. A spokesman for Plaid Cymru said to reporters, 'We have turned the invitation down in view of the Minister's general attitude towards Wales'.

364 Princess Diana was plagued by paparazzi, who followed her daily. When The Queen called 21 newspaper editors to a meeting to request some privacy for the beleaguered Princess, Barry Askew of *News of the World* commented that if Diana didn't wish to be photographed, she should ask a servant to run her errands. The Queen told him that he was 'extremely pompous'.

365 In 2012 sneaky pictures emerged of Prince Harry at a 'naked party' in a hotel room in Las Vegas. The media went crazy about the story of a group of men inviting a group of women to a party – although surely the real news story was: why had the Prince's staff not carried out security checks?

366 While on a skiing holiday in Klosters in 2005 Prince Charles was asked to take part in an official photo shoot and interview. Not realising he was close to a live microphone, the exasperated heir to the throne was overheard complaining about the squad of waiting journalists.

367 In 2010 Sarah, Duchess of York, was caught in a media 'sting'. Mazher Mahmood, an undercover reporter for *News of the World,* pretended to be an overseas businessman looking for investment partners. A year later, the newspaper was closed down, following an investigation into its shameful practices.

368 Shortly after the wedding of Prince William and Catherine Middleton, French magazine *Closer* published topless photographs of the Duchess, taken with a long lens while she was at a private villa. The Prince, who has studied privacy law in detail, fought back. In 2017 a French judge found *Closer* magazine guilty of 'unjustified intrusion'.

369 In 1985 the *Daily Mirror* revealed that Princess Michael of Kent's father had been a Nazi officer in Hitler's SS. The Queen's press secretary Michael Shea released a statement saying that the news came as 'a total shock' to the Princess, yet the statement also said she had 'confirmed tonight that it is true that her father was a member of the SS'.

370 In 2012 a phone 'prank' directed at the Royal Family went tragically wrong. While the pregnant Duchess of Cambridge was in hospital with severe morning sickness, an Australian radio DJ made a hoax call pretending to be The Queen. The nurse who answered transferred the call to a colleague, who unwittingly revealed details of the Duchess's condition live on air. The poor nurse who had answered the call, and been taken in by the hoax, was so distraught that she took her own life.

ELIZABETH'S WORLD

119

Ten social milestones

Britain has seen huge changes since the 1950s – it seems almost inconceivable now that when The Queen came to the throne there was no state-funded university education, same-sex couples were forbidden to marry, and there was no speed limit on the brand new M1!

371 Britain's cities had been notorious for their filthy air since the 19th century. In 1952 London practically ground to a halt as unusual weather conditions and factory smoke combined into the lethal Great London Smog. It was estimated that between 8,000 and 12,000 people died, and many thousands more suffered breathing problems. This spurred on the first Clean Air Act of 1956.

372 The country's first full-length motorway, the M1, was opened in 1959, at first with no lighting or speed limit. After a slew of accidents, a speed limit of 70 mph was imposed in 1965.

373 In 1963 the Robbins Report paved the way for state-funded higher education, enabling students from

Opposite page: (top left and right) In 1953, smog masks were all the rage in London, due to health-threatening levels of air pollution. (Bottom) The death penalty was abolished in 1969 after years of protests such as this one, photographed in 1935 outside Wandsworth Prison, London.

Below: A baby is weighed in a newly opened NHS clinic in Bristol, July 1948. The NHS has grown dramatically during The Queen's reign.

all backgrounds to attend university, regardless of their financial situation. Until student funding was announced, only the wealthiest people in the country had been able to have a university education.

374 On 8 November 1969 it was decreed that British courts could no longer order the death penalty for murder – this effectively brought to an end the death penalty in Britain. Previous changes in the law had meant that the only crimes still punishable by death had been murder, piracy with violence, and treason. (The death penalty for the latter two was abolished in 1998.)

375 In 1967 two new laws were passed, changing the lives of women and of homosexual men in England, Wales and Scotland. The 1967 Abortion Act allowed doctors in Great Britain to perform abortions, as long as strict criteria were met. The 1967 Sexual Offences Act decriminalised sexual acts in private between two consenting men over the age of 21. Neither of the Acts, however, was passed in Northern Ireland.

376 The 1969 Divorce Reform Act meant that for the first time neither partner had to prove that the 'fault' lay with their spouse. Although many religious leaders criticised the new Act, it helped to end years of misery for people trapped in unhappy marriages.

377 The National Health Service, or NHS, was arguably the single most important of all the social milestones of The Queen's lifetime. It began officially in 1947, but grew dramatically in the early years of her reign. A state-funded scheme open to all was the idea of a brilliant Welsh politician, Aneurin 'Nye' Bevan, the Minister for Health in Clement Attlee's post-war government.

378 The Race Relations Act of 1965 was the first piece of legislation in the UK to address racial discrimination, on 'the grounds of colour, race or ethnic or national origins in public places'. It was strengthened in 1968 to cover employment and housing, and in 1976 the Commission for Racial Equality was established.

379 The Queen's reign saw the explosion of a modern 'Aid Industry', which paired increasingly

intimate media coverage of disasters with the awareness-raising power of celebrity. As a horrified world watched a famine devastate Ethiopia in 1984, rock star Bob Geldof, frustrated by the slowness of the big aid agencies to respond, kick-started a fund-raising initiative. He appealed directly to showbiz friends and fellow stars to help. The Band Aid single *Do They Know It's Christmas* was the Christmas no. 1 of 1984, and the Live Aid concert of 1985 was the world's biggest rock concert. In total, over £30 million was raised.

380 In 2004, after a very long campaign, same-sex couples were granted the right to enter into a Civil Partnership. While the change was welcome, greater joy greeted the 2014 law permitting 'equal marriage', between same-sex couples. These laws applied in Scotland, England, and Wales, but not in Northern Ireland.

Technological breakthroughs

Over her many years as monarch, The Queen has witnessed extraordinary technological advances. British scientists, engineers and inventors have often been at the forefront of these discoveries.

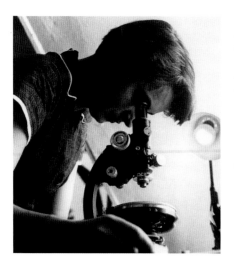

381 In the early 1950s, scientist Rosalind Franklin (above), at King's College in London, obtained images of DNA using X-ray crystallography. Her images enabled fellow scientists James Watson and Francis Crick to create their double-helix model of DNA. On 25 April 1953 Watson and Crick published their discovery. The two men, and a third colleague, Maurice Wilkins, were jointly awarded the Nobel Prize in Physiology or Medicine; Rosalind Franklin's essential contribution was not rewarded.

382 On 22 September 1955 the first independent television company in Britain began broadcasting. This ended the previous monopoly of the British Broadcasting Corporation (BBC). The start of commercial television began with the Independent Television Authority, known as 'ITA'.

383 In 1956 The Queen opened the first nuclear power station in Britain, Calder Hall. It was the first nuclear power station in the world to be able to supply a substantial quantity of electrical power to the national grid. In 1957 Britain tested its first hydrogen bomb.

384 The arrival of the contraceptive pill in the 1960s meant that women could finally take control of how many children they had. In 1974 the first family planning clinics were set up, making the pill available more widely (initially GPs had been reluctant to prescribe it to unmarried or young women).

385 The first official British space programme began in the year Queen Elizabeth II came to the throne. Seven years later, in 1959, Britain began its satellite project. *Ariel*, the first British satellite, was launched in 1962. The National Space Centre was set up in 1985.

386 In December 1967 the world's first heart transplant was performed in South Africa by Dr Christaan Barnard. Sadly, the patient, Louis Washkansky, only lived for 18 days after his operation, dying of pneumonia. Less than six months later, the first heart transplant in Britain was performed at the National Heart Hospital in London, by South African-born surgeon, Donald Ross. The patient, Frederick West, died 46 days later, from an infection.

387 When a baby girl was born in Oldham, Greater Manchester, on 25 July 1978, her birth made history. Louise Brown was conceived outside

Opposite page: **The Queen views the reactor charging floor as she officially opens Calder Hall in Cumbria in 1956, the world's first atomic power station to be connected to the national grid.**

Left, from top: **Internet guru Tim Berners-Lee; the contraceptive pill; Dolly the sheep, the first genetically created animal, meets the press in 1997.**

her mother's body, and became known as the world's first 'test tube baby'. The process was pioneered by gynaecologist Patrick Steptoe and physiologist Robert Edwards. Louise's birth paved the way for in-vitro fertilisation, or IVF.

388 In 1997 a belated birth announcement was released: Dolly the sheep had been cloned in July 1996, at the Roslin Institute in Midlothian, Scotland. Dolly lived until the age of 6.

389 The American phone company Motorola was the very first company to create a hand-held mobile

phone – back in 1973. The first mobile phone call made in the UK was on 1 January 1985 on the Vodafone network.

390 In 1989 British scientist Tim Berners-Lee helped develop the world wide web, later known as the internet. Berners-Lee was born in London to parents who were computer scientists. However, in an interview he revealed that his love of technology began simply as a love of trains: 'I made some electronic gadgets to control the trains. Then I ended up getting more interested in electronics than trains. Later on, when I was in college I made a computer out of an old television set.'

Disasters and dark moments

As monarch, The Queen has shared the grief of her people on many sad occasions. It has often been difficult for her to maintain the expected poise when hearing stories of loss and heartbreak.

391 The North Sea Flood between 31 January and 1 February 1953 caused death and devastation across eastern England and the Netherlands. Hurricane-force winds caused a storm surge of water which destroyed sea defences, homes and farmland, and battered areas still trying to cope with the damage caused by wartime bombings.

392 On 21 October 1966 the small Welsh coal-mining village of Aberfan was devastated by a fatal avalanche of coal-mining debris. One of the worst-hit buildings was the village school. In total 116 children and 23 adults were killed. The Queen visited the village, where she was served tea inside the home of a Mrs Beatrice Williams, who said The Queen was 'very upset'. Mrs Williams's granddaughter gave The Queen a posy and a card bearing the heartbreaking message 'from the remaining children of Aberfan'.

393 There have been a number of rail disasters during Queen Elizabeth II's reign, and her first decade was particularly terrible. In 1952 the Harrow and Wealdstone crash killed 112 people and injured more than 300 others. In 1955 five major rail crashes occurred, and two years later 90 people were killed and 173 injured in a crash at Lewisham, East London.

394 In late April 1986 a nuclear reactor at Chernobyl power station exploded. The Soviet government in Moscow was reluctant to release information to the media, but reports of radiation contamination began to flood in from neighbouring countries. The official death toll was given as 31 – the number of people killed directly by the explosion. Scientists are still divided as to how many people really died, with the most conservative estimates at around 10,000 people.

395 The *Herald of Free Enterprise* was a car ferry operating between Zeebrugge, in Belgium, and Dover, in England. On 6 March 1987 the ferry capsized just outside Zeebrugge port, killing 193 passengers and crew. The accident, caused by human error, remains one of Britain's worst maritime disasters in peacetime. The Queen awarded three Queen's Gallantry Medals and two George Medals (one posthumously) to those who helped save others.

A number 30 double-decker bus blown apart in Holborn, central London, in the terrorist attack on 7 July 2005.

Ocean, which hit 14 countries in South-East Asia. At least 275,000 people, British holidaymakers among them, are known to have been killed by the tsunami and five million people were affected, losing their families, homes and possessions. The Queen made what was described as a 'substantial donation' to the emergency fundraising.

398 In the hot summer of 2011 riots erupted in cities and towns across England. Protests started in Tottenham, north London, after police shot and killed a man on 4 August. In the aftermath, what began as a peaceful demonstration turned into violent rioting, looting and arson across the country. The riots finally subsided on 12 August – when it began to rain.

399 On 7 July 2005, four suicide bombers detonated bombs on London transport, killing 56 people and injuring hundreds. The Queen said to the country: 'Atrocities such as these simply reinforce our sense of community, our humanity and our trust in the rule of law.' When a horrific terror attack took place in Manchester in 2017, The Queen visited injured young people in hospital, and said publicly: 'I would like to express my admiration for the way the people of Manchester have responded, with humanity and compassion, to this act of barbarity.'

400 On 14 June 2017 fire ravaged Grenfell Tower, a 27-storey residential council block situated in the west London Royal Borough of Kensington and Chelsea. Despite heroic efforts of emergency services, 71 people died and a horrifying story of council neglect and cost cutting emerged. Two days after the fire The Queen and Prince William visited an emergency shelter. The Prince described the fire site as 'one of the most terrible things I have ever seen'. Photographs showed The Queen close to tears as she spoke to charity workers and volunteers.

396 The 1989 FA cup semi-final on 15 April was one of the worst days in sporting history. Early in the match between Liverpool and Nottingham Forest at the Hillsborough Stadium in Sheffield, severe overcrowding in the central pens led to hundreds of supporters being crushed. Ninety-six people died and almost 800 were injured.

397 On 26 December 2004 an earthquake registering 9.2 in magnitude occurred off the Indonesian coastline. It caused a tsunami in the Indian

Ten members of The Queen's household staff

Have you ever wanted to walk in The Queen's shoes? Or look after her swans?
Then there could be a job opportunity in the Royal Household for you!

401 The Master of the Horse (a ceremonial role) is required to be present at all state occasions when The Queen is on a horse or riding in a horse-drawn carriage. The Master is also in charge of the Royal Stables and the Royal Mews.

402 The archaic-sounding Queen's Flag Sergeant is actually one of the newest roles in the Royal Household. It is held, normally for a couple of years, by a serving soldier, who is responsible for ensuring that all flags on royal homes and vehicles are flown correctly. He or she sees to it that the Royal Standard is raised, to indicate at which home The Queen is in residence, and that it is lowered when she leaves.

403 A new Master of The Queen's Music is appointed every decade, with this 500-year-old role being awarded to an eminent musician. In 2014 The Queen chose Scottish composer Judith Weir, the first woman to be appointed.

404 At the height of her fervour for all things Scottish, Queen Victoria created a new role within the Royal Household: Piper to the Sovereign. The tradition continues: at 9am every weekday the Piper plays for approximately 15 minutes under The Queen's window – as long as she is in residence at Windsor Castle, Buckingham Palace, Balmoral or the Palace of Holyroodhouse.

405 The Queen's grandfather King George V was a keen philatelist, and The Queen inherited a very valuable stamp collection from him (via her father). The Keeper of The Queen's Stamps is responsible for the historic collection, as well as curating the modern collection, which focuses mostly on stamps from Britain and the Commonwealth.

406 The Keeper of the Privy Purse has responsibility for the monarch's private expenses. One Keeper featured in a letter written by poet Ted Hughes describing a meeting with The

Queen in 1974: 'We sat down, & the Keeper of the Privy Purse appeared, jovial fellow, who poured out glasses of sherry. He said The Queen had been reading my books and had discovered words that she didn't know were in the English language, & she wanted to ask me about them.'

407 The role of The Queen's Bargemaster was created in 1215, when most of the monarch's travelling was on the river. The Bargemaster is among the most ancient roles within the Royal Household, and includes commanding a fleet of 24 Royal Watermen.

408 The Queen is the owner of every 'unclaimed' mute swan in open waters in England and Wales. For over 700 years one of the most prestigious roles in the Royal Household was that of Keeper of the Swans. In 1993 the job was divided into two new roles: The Warden of the Swans and The Marker of the Swans. They have responsibility for the care of all Her Majesty's swans on the River Thames.

409 The Royal Horological Conservator has responsibility for all of The Queen's timepieces – and she owns around a thousand! When a new horologist was required in 2013, the job vacancy stated that the right person must be 'experienced at working with hand and machine tools' and able to 'strip and clean mechanisms [and] make new parts'.

410 The Royal Shoe-Wearer literally gets to walk in The Queen's shoes. Being the monarch requires not only being stylish, but also wearing practical clothing, including shoes that don't pinch or cause blisters. So The Queen has someone with exactly the same size feet as she does, to break in her shoes for her.

Soundtrack to a reign

In 1977 the Sex Pistols' second single *God Save The Queen* reached the top of the charts in the UK. While The Queen's image hasn't featured on many other record sleeves since the 1950s (and she probably hasn't heard most of the records), her reign has seen some iconic album releases.

411 The Beatles' eighth album, *Sergeant Pepper's Lonely Hearts Club Band*, was released on 1 June 1967 and hailed by DJs as the soundtrack to the 'Summer of Love'. A reviewer for *NME* wrote: 'Trust the Beatles to come up with something different!'

412 *The Rise and Fall of Ziggy Stardust and the Spiders from Mars* (better known simply as 'Ziggy Stardust') was released on 16 June 1972. The concept album tells the story of David Bowie's alter ego. In an interview some years later, Bowie explained: 'What I did with my Ziggy Stardust was package a totally credible, plastic rock & roll singer … And that was what was needed at the time.'

413 *The Dark Side of the Moon* by Pink Floyd was released on 1 March 1973. For the album cover, the band requested something 'simple and bold'. The cover has become one of the best-known album artworks of all time; it was designed by English graphic designer Storm Thorgerson, of the design group Hipgnosis.

STEREO

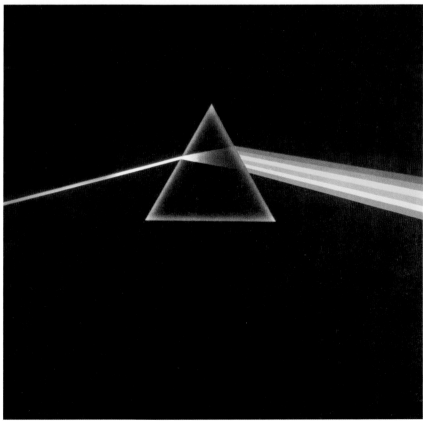

Opposite page: **Punk band the Sex Pistols sign a new record contract in front of Buckingham Palace before the release of their single,** *God Save The Queen.* **Left to right: John Lydon, Steve Jones, Paul Cook and Sid Vicious.**

This page: **Arguably the first concept album, The Beatles'** *Sgt Pepper* **in 1967 'ushered in the summer of love', while Pink Floyd's** *Dark Side of the Moon* **in 1973 explored insanity. (Below) Manchester band The Smiths, photographed in 1985 on the release of their second album,** *Meat is Murder.*

414 1977 was the year of The Queen's Silver Jubilee, with street parties, flag waving and expressions of national pride. It was also the defining year of Punk. The Sex Pistols' only album, *Never Mind The Bollocks Here's The Sex Pistols*, was causing enjoyable outrage, while the group was banned from playing live in many venues and from appearing on live television. The album's controversial title also meant that it appeared as a blank space on many official music sales lists.

415 Manchester band The Smiths defined a generation of deep-thinking Indie teens. Front man Morrissey became a media sensation – alternately

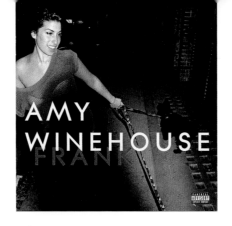

loved and hated, but always making
headlines. The Smiths' iconic second
album *Meat is Murder* was released in
1985, and reached no. 1 in the UK charts.
Thirty years later, in 2015, it was described
by *Uncut* as 'a radical manifesto for
troubled times'.

416 George Michael burst onto the
British music scene in pop duo
Wham!, who sold more than 30 million
records. In 1987 he made his solo debut
with *Faith*, winning a Grammy for 'Album
of the Year'.

417 The 1990s Britpop phenomenon
was dominated by Oasis,
followed closely by rivals Blur. With
Definitely Maybe (1994), Oasis shot to
the top of the album charts, making it
the fastest-selling debut album of all time.

418 The debut album by The
Spice Girls was released
on the Virgin label on 19 September
1996. *Spice* made it to no. 1
in the album charts in 17
countries; in 1997 alone it
sold over 19 million copies.
Girl Power had arrived!

419 *Frank* (2003), Amy Winehouse's
debut album, was a slow burner,
but within five years, she had become a
star, and *Frank* was certified as triple
platinum. In an early interview, Amy said
of *Frank*: 'While I have written about times
in my life that have given me trouble and
there are points on the album where I am
really upset and really angry, I'll always put
a punch-line in there and I'll always make
it funny.'

420 In early 21st-century style,
Adele was talent spotted on
MySpace and given a recording contract.
Her second album, *21*, released in 2011,
won a record six Grammy Awards, two Brit
Awards and three American Music Awards.
21 has sold over 30 million copies around
the world, and has made the girl from West
Norwood, London, an international star.

Villains and scandals

Britain's most prolific serial killer, the Moor's Murderers, the Great Train Robbery and the 'Cambridge Spies' … The Queen's reign has seen some infamous criminals, who were (mostly) brought to justice.

421 Ruth Ellis was the last woman in Britain to be hanged, convicted of murdering her abusive lover, David Blakely. His violence included beating her until she had a miscarriage, shortly after which Ellis shot Blakely outside a pub in north London. Then she calmly told bystanders to call the police, to whom she gave herself up. Her execution on 13 July 1955 caused a public outcry, contributing to the abolition of the death penalty for murder.

422 In the 1960s, post was taken by special Royal Mail train from Glasgow to London overnight. On board were a sorting office and a special carriage dedicated to 'high value items'. On the night of 8 August 1963 a gang of masked men decoyed the train and attacked the workers. They stole over £2 million. The 'Great Train Robbery' has been romanticised, even though the gang viciously attacked the driver, Jack Mills, who died seven years later from head injuries sustained during the robbery.

423 In May 1951 civil servants Guy Burgess and Donald Maclean disappeared from their government offices. Five years later the two men were discovered living in Moscow and revealed as Communist members of a spy ring known as the Cambridge Spies. In 1979 it was revealed that this had included the late art historian Sir Anthony Blunt, a distant cousin of the Queen Mother. He had held the royal appointment of Surveyor of The King's Pictures since 1945 and worked for The Queen until 1962.

424 In 1961 the Secretary of State for War was John Profumo, aged 45 (and married); he began a relationship with 19-year-old Christine Keeler. The government panicked because Keeler was also believed to be the lover of Yevgeny Ivanov, a naval attaché for the Soviet

Opposite page: **Christine Keeler leaving the Old Bailey in 1963. (Below) In April 2015 raiders drilled through a vault wall in London's Hatton Garden and stole millions of pounds worth of jewels and cash.**

This page, from top: **Moors murderers Ian Brady and Myra Hindley, 1966; Ruth Ellis; Lord Lucan; and Sir Anthony Blunt, Surveyor of the Queen's Pictures until revealed as a spy in 1979.**

Union. The ensuing scandal and court case became known as the Profumo Affair. The society osteopath Stephen Ward, who introduced them, committed suicide before his trial, Profumo's parliamentary career came to an end – and Keeler ended up in prison for perjury during another trial in 1963.

425 On the night of 7 November 1974 a young woman named Sandra Rivett was murdered. She was a nanny working for the family of Lord and Lady Lucan. It is believed that, in the dark house, Lord Lucan mistook Rivett for his estranged wife, and killed her. He then attacked his wife and left her for dead before fleeing. The mystery of his disappearance has never been solved.

426 On Friday 12 August 1966 three unarmed policemen were shot dead on a residential street in west London by known criminals Harry Roberts, John Duddy and John Witney, who were later captured and imprisoned. In summing up, the judge described the murders as 'the most heinous crime to have been committed in this country for a generation or more'.

427 On 5 November 1991 newspaper mogul Robert Maxwell was found drowned, floating in the water near his luxury yacht. Initially, tributes poured in – until it was discovered that Maxwell had defrauded his company's pension fund of £440 million, affecting around 30,000 of his employees.

428 Sadly, many distressing murder cases have come to light since 1952. Amongst the most notorious murderers are Dennis Nilson, Myra Hindley and Ian Brady, and Peter Sutcliffe. Many of these prosecutions and cases have led to changes in the law and the way prosecutions are conducted, including 67 changes in practice or law made as a result of the flawed inquiry into the murder of Stephen Lawrence.

429 In 2000 a family doctor named Harold Shipman was convicted of murdering at least 250 of his patients – he may have killed even more. His killing spree seems to have begun in 1975 and continued for the next 23 years, until he was arrested. He is Britain's most prolific serial killer. Shipman hanged himself in his prison cell in 2004.

430 In April 2015 a gang of criminals, nicknamed 'the granddads' gang' because of their advanced ages, carried out an audacious burglary at the Hatton Garden Safe Deposit Company, in the heart of London's diamond trade. The thieves entered via a lift shaft, then drilled through the reinforced walls; they stole goods worth up to £200 million. In 2016 seven men were found guilty and sentenced to prison.

Ten British fashion designers

Princesses Elizabeth and Margaret Rose flew the flag of British fashion around the world, and the new Queen Elizabeth II continued to champion British designers. Throughout her reign, fashion has evolved – gaining a conscience and using revolutionary ideas.

431 **Norman Hartnell** made his first dress for Princess Elizabeth in 1935, when she was a bridesmaid at her uncle's wedding. Hartnell's designs for her wedding and coronation made his name internationally famous. Although he and The Queen usually favoured bright colours, in 1956 Hartnell created a black evening dress, for a film premiere. He knew the stars would be dressed in glitzy clothing, so Her Majesty would stand out in black.

432 Sir Edwin Hardy Amies, known simply as **Hardy Amies**, was The Queen's official dressmaker from 1952 until his retirement in 1989. He understood the monarch's need to dress stylishly *and* suitably for each specific occasion. He was knighted in 1993.

433 While still a student at the Royal College of Art, **Marion Foale** submitted a design for The Queen's Mantle, to be worn at the annual Order of the British Empire dedication ceremony. Her design won the competition – and has been used throughout The Queen's reign.

434 **Mary Quant** was at the vanguard of the Swinging Sixties. She created the mini skirt and hotpants and was *the* fashion icon of 1960s London. Quant gave young people the chance to dress differently from their parents – a radical idea at the time – and was quoted as saying 'Fashion is a tool to compete in life outside the home'. In 1966 she was awarded an OBE and in 2015 she was made a Dame.

435 **Vivienne Westwood** burst onto the British fashion scene as *the* Punk designer, and was in a relationship with Malcolm McLaren, the Sex Pistols' manager. Her early designs included slashed clothing, bondage trousers and a liberal use of safety-pins. In 1971 Westwood and McLaren set up their first boutique, 'Sex', in the King's Road, but by the 1980s Westwood had gone solo and built a fashion empire. She received an OBE in 1992 and was made a Dame in 2006 – but she has never dressed The Queen! She did, however, take inspiration from the Diamond Jubilee for her 2012 collection.

436 **Katherine Hamnett** defined the youth movement of the 1980s with her socially conscious designs, often

Opposite page: **(left)** Sir Hardy Amies and models in 1953. **(Right)** Marion Foale with her design for The Queen's Mantle.

This page: **(left)** Sixties star designer Mary Quant gets a trendy haircut from super stylist Vidal Sassoon. **(Below)** One to watch: The Queen and Anna Wintour, Editor of American *Vogue*, view Richard Quinn's catwalk show before presenting him with the inaugural Queen Elizabeth II award for British Design in February 2018.

Right: **Designer Vivienne Westwood in her studio.**
Below: **Paul Smith at the launch of his exhibition** *Hello, my name is Paul Smith* **at the London Design Museum in November 2013.**

Opposite page: **The newly wed Catherine, Duchess of Cambridge leaves Westminster Abbey in her beautiful dress designed by Sarah Burton at Alexander McQueen.**

bearing slogans that were anti-war, pro-the environment, anti-nuclear and pro-gay rights. Her 'Choose Life' T-shirt, inspired by Buddhist philosophy, was made famous by the pop group Wham! and became associated with the fight against HIV/Aids. Hamnett's label specialises in sustainable clothing, and her activism is alive and kicking.

437 Stella McCartney, daughter of ex-Beatle Paul McCartney and his photographer wife Linda, worked as an intern for Christian Lacroix and studied fashion at Central Saint Martins in London. The collection she produced for her graduation show was modelled by supermodel friends, including Naomi Campbell and Kate Moss.

438 While still in his twenties, Alexander McQueen was made Chief Designer at Givenchy. Five years later he set up his eponymous fashion label. McQueen's brilliant, groundbreaking designs saw him named British Designer of the Year four times. Tragically, in 2010 McQueen committed suicide. His label, Alexander McQueen, is favoured by several younger members of the Royal Family, including the Duchess of Cambridge, who wore an Alexander McQueen wedding dress.

439 In 1997 Matthew Williamson's debut fashion show, Electric Angels, precipitated him into the spotlight – helped by the presence of several prominent supermodels on his catwalk. In 2004 he opened his flagship store on Bruton Street in London – the same road on which The Queen was born.

440 As a teenager, Paul Smith was intent on being a professional racing cyclist – but his dreams were shattered when he was injured in a crash at the age of 17. After months in hospital he started working in a fashion boutique, which led to an interest in design. He opened his first shop in 1970 and launched his first collection in 1976. He has become an international fashion icon, and was knighted by The Queen in 2009.

ELIZABETH CELEBRATED

The image of Queen Elizabeth II is instantly recognisable, not just in Britain but all over the world. She has been captured 'officially' in commissioned (although not always flattering) portraits, and unofficially, in (even less flattering) cartoons. The Queen has been portrayed by actors on stage and screen and mimicked by countless comedians. Her face has been celebrated on stamps and coins from around the globe, and on some cheeky items of royal memorabilia. However, long after these have vanished, her name will endure, on the bridges, buildings, ships and even islands that have been named in her honour.

Queen Elizabeth II by
Andy Warhol, 1985
(see page 144).

Ten royal portraits

The Queen's likeness has been captured thousands of times;
these are ten of our favourite portraits, which each seem to reveal
a different aspect of this most private of monarchs.

441 When Princess Elizabeth was 7, her parents commissioned Philip de Laszlo (1869–1937) to paint her portrait (left). The Hungarian artist had already painted the Princess's mother twice, to great acclaim. He painted a beautiful portrait of the young princess in a flowing white dress; her face is easily recognisable as the future Queen Elizabeth II.

442 Cecil Beaton (1904–1980) photographed the Princess in 1945 (above), and described the event with his customary flamboyance: 'I was bidden to the Palace to see the Princess's dresses … Of all those we photographed … the most successful was the pink spangled crinoline which was one of her mother's pre-war dresses, now altered to fit the daughter'. Beaton was a favourite of the Queen Mother's and worked as a royal photographer for over 40 years. Key assignments included that of official photographer of The Queen's coronation (see also page 63).

443 Dorothy Wilding (1893–1976) was the first woman to hold the appointment of Official Royal Photographer. She had taken her first royal portrait in 1928, but her first official assignment was the 1937 coronation of King George VI and Queen Elizabeth. Wilding began as an apprentice to photographer Marian Neilson before opening her own studios, in London and New York. Her earliest photographs of Queen Elizabeth were taken in 1952. The hand-coloured print (right) is one of a series from that first shoot. Arguably, Wilding helped promote the most iconic image of The Queen, as this picture was hung in offices all over the Commonwealth.

444 In 1954 The Queen was painted by Australian artist Sir William Dargie (1912–2003). She wore a diamond tiara, a present from her grandmother, Queen Mary, and a dress designed by Norman Hartnell. The dress was of gold

tulle decorated with a wattle motif, so the painting has become known as 'the wattle portrait'. The Queen liked it so much she asked Dargie to paint a copy for her.

445 Polish Expressionist painter Feliks Topolski (1907–1989) was commissioned by Prince Philip to create a mural (previous page) depicting scenes from the coronation. Topolski, who was born in Warsaw, moved to London in the 1930s to paint a record of King George V's Silver Jubilee. He worked as an official war artist during the Second World War and became a well-respected figure in the London art world. His coronation mural is in 14 friezes.

446 Italian artist Pietro Annigoni (1910–1988) painted *Queen Regent* in 1955 and *Her Majesty in Robes of the British Empire* in 1969 (above, left). In 1972 he painted The Queen and the Duke of Edinburgh for their silver wedding anniversary. Annigoni also painted a poignantly wistful painting of Princess Margaret, following her separation from the man she had wanted to marry, Captain Peter Townsend. The artist captured perfectly the sadness of The Queen's sister at that moment in her life.

447 A series entitled *Reigning Queens* 1985 by Andy Warhol (1928–1987) includes portraits of four queens: Queen Elizabeth II, Queen Beatrix of the Netherlands, Queen Margrethe II of Denmark and Queen Ntombi Twala of eSwatini (formerly Swaziland). The artist, who died two years after painting the series, once said, 'I want to be as famous as the Queen of England'. In 2012 the Royal Collection Trust bought four of Warhol's images of The Queen.

448 To commemorate the Golden Jubilee, the Commonwealth Secretariat commissioned a new portrait of The Queen by Nigerian artist Chinwe Chukwuogo-Roy (1952–2012), photographed in front of her full-length portrait (above), which depicts The Queen dressed in a floor-length dress of bright purple, surrounded by a landscape painted in jewel-like colours.

449 In 2004 Canadian photographer Chris Levine unveiled his unusual portrait, *Lightness of Being* (2007) (right). It depicts The Queen wearing a glittering diamond crown, but with her eyes closed. A version of the portrait, known as *Equanimity*, was used on the cover of *Time* magazine in June 2012. To produce the work, Levine used a camera that moved around The Queen on a circular track. In an interview, Levine said: 'Her Majesty is a seasoned and highly professional model. She was completely obliging and was very patient.'

450 In 2012 Australian-born artist Ralph Heimans painted a portrait of The Queen at night (left) standing contemplatively in Westminster Abbey, at the precise spot where she was crowned. The large painting, measuring 11 × 9 ft, was entitled *The Coronation Theatre, Westminster Abbey: Portrait of Her Majesty Queen Elizabeth II*. It was purchased by Westminster Abbey – an institution that rarely buys new works of art.

Ten unofficial 'portraits'

Compared to some of her predecessors (Queen Victoria, for example), Elizabeth II has come off fairly lightly at the hands of satirical artists and cartoonists, as this affectionate selection demonstrates.

451

'The Sporting Life' by Marc (Mark Boxer) hints at The Queen's abiding passion!

452

Naturally The Queen had a puppet character that popped up, with headscarf and tiara, on the popular satirical *Spitting Image* television programme.

454

'The Royal Barge', by Andy Davey of *The Sun*, with Prince Harry waterskiing behind the Royal Barge, anticipated the Diamond Jubilee river pageant of 2012.

453

A well-known Pearly Queen and her Prince Consort were captured by cartoonist Trog for this 1977 issue of *Punch* magazine.

'How terribly exciting, Philip, dear. They're making a film called "Helen Mirren" and I've been offered the part.'

455

Helen Mirren's portrayal of The Queen (see also overleaf) is considered to be one of the best.

456

The Queen knights tennis star Andy Murray with a racket in 2016, with Prime Minister David Cameron approving.

457 Gerald Scarfe's portrait of The Queen, from his first-ever selling exhibition in 1988.

458 The Queen wears a '50's nifty' badge and waves a sceptre in this American Golden Jubilee caricature of 2002.

459 The cartoonist Wally Fawkes, better known as Trog, was commissioned to produce a caricature for The Queen's Golden Jubilee. Inspired by a visit to the *Eastenders* set, he showed her pulling pints behind the bar of the Queen Vic!

460 This cheeky 'Kiss One Quick' mug was designed by Simon Drew and made by Mclaggan Smith for the Diamond Jubilee.

Actors who have played The Queen

It's an impressive list, which includes The Queen herself!!

461 When Prince Charles was watching the 2012 Olympics Opening Ceremony in London, he was as stunned as everyone else in the audience to discover that 'The Queen' in the James Bond video was his mother, not an actor! According to Lord Coe, even the heir to the throne and his sons had been kept out of the secret. They all roared with laughter; Prince Charles exclaimed 'My God! It really is The Queen!' and Princes William and Harry called out 'Go, Granny!'

462 In the film *The Queen* (2006), Her Majesty was portrayed by actor **Dame Helen Mirren** and the script was written by Peter Morgan (who also wrote *The Audience* and *The Crown*). In an interview for *Vanity Fair*, Mirren commented: 'The Queen has been in my life longer than any other person apart from my elder sister, so she has been absolutely consistently in my life.'

463 In 2010 playwright Moira Buffini premiered a one-act play for the Tricycle Theatre, a fringe theatre in London.

Above: **The cast of the extended version of *Handbagged* perform at the Vaudeville Theatre in London, 2014.**

Below: **Actor Jeannette Charles, playing The Queen in Austin Powers, 2002.**

Handbagged was about the relationship between The Queen and Margaret Thatcher. In 2014 an extended version of *Handbagged* transferred to the Vaudeville Theatre in London's West End, to great acclaim. The younger and older Elizabeth II were played by **Lucy Robinson** and **Marion Bailey** respectively. Bailey had played the younger Queen in the 2010 version.

464 Dame Helen Mirren reprised her role as The Queen in the stage play *The Audience* in 2013. It was performed at The Gielgud Theatre in London before transferring to Broadway in New York. *The Audience* is about the monarch's weekly meeting with her Prime Ministers. In 2015 actress **Kristin Scott-Thomas**, who had recently been made a Dame, reprised the role of The Queen.

465 In 2016 Netflix captured the spotlight with its blockbusting series *The Crown*. The Queen was first played by **Clare Foy**, with the Duke of Edinburgh played by Matt Smith (formerly most famous as Doctor Who!). In an interview, Foy talked about her experience of becoming The Queen: 'I feel a lot of sympathy for her, and the longer I've worked on this the more my admiration for her has grown.'

466 *A Royal Night Out* (2015) portrayed the night of the VE celebrations, when the young princesses were allowed out to mingle with the crowds. More fiction than fact, it featured a burgeoning, if short-lived, romance. The film starred **Sarah Gordon** as Princess Elizabeth and Bel Powley as Princess Margaret.

467 **Jeannette Charles** has made an entire career of playing The Queen, most memorably in *Austin Powers* (2002), in which she knights hero Powers for services to The Queen. Other appearances as a rather comic Queen

'The Queen' makes a dramatic entrance, parachuting into the stadium during the opening ceremony of the 2012 Olympic Games.

Below: Helen Mirren in an award-winning portrayal in *The Queen*, 2006.

Elizabeth II include *Naked Gun* (1988) and National Lampoon's *European Vacation* (1985).

468 The then child actor Freya Wilson made a brief appearance as the young Princess Elizabeth in *The King's Speech* (2010). Princesses Elizabeth and Margaret appear in a cosy domestic scene with their father (Colin Firth) and mother (Helena Bonham Carter) before the pressures of sovereignty descend on them all.

469 Tony award-winning American actor Jane Alexander played The Queen in the TV movie *A Royal Romance* (2011). The film imagined her overseeing the wedding of her grandson Prince William. It aired four months after the royal wedding, relying on American fascination with the British Royal Family.

470 A cartoon version of The Queen has even featured on the outrageous US TV cult series *Family Guy*! Actor Cate Blanchett provided the voice for Her Majesty, who made a brief appearance in the episode 'Viewer Mail#2'.

The Queen's head

478

The Queen's image has adorned literally billions of stamps and coins in a huge variety of denominations, pounds, dollars, rupees, kina, mils and shillings carrying the most recognisable, reproduced face in world history.

472

472

476

471

471 Her Majesty's first appearance on a stamp was in 1932, on a 6 cents value of Newfoundland. The youthful princess continued to appear on the stamps of Australia, Canada and South Africa, and even on a triangular stamp from New Zealand. Ironically, she didn't appear on a British stamp until she became Queen in 1952.

472 British commemorative stamps are issued about every three weeks now, but in 1953 just one set was authorised, for the coronation. The designer Edmund Dulac created four classic stamps. His one shilling and threepence value was unique for depicting The Queen facing the viewer.

473 The gold sovereign was long a symbol of British economic power. After a gap of 40 years, bullion sovereigns began to be issued again in 1957. In 1989 the 500th anniversary of the coin was marked by the minting of a special 'medieval' sovereign, with The Queen enthroned like a Tudor monarch.

474 One of the rarest of The Queen's stamps is the £1 value chocolate and violet from Jamaica, planned for 1956 but never issued. Nearly all stocks were withdrawn and destroyed, so that today only seven copies are thought to exist. The stamp depicts cigar rolling, hardly an appropriate topic to commemorate today.

475 The Royal Maundy is a curious legacy of ancient origin. Each year, just before Good Friday, Her Majesty distributes little silver Maundy coins in denominations of 4, 3, 2 pence and a penny to pensioners in combinations of value that match her age. The penny coin is only 11 mm in diameter. The coins always depict the head of the young Elizabeth on the obverse, and are legal tender, though you will never find them in your change.

476 The largest, most intrinsically valuable coin in the world, and the biggest to depict The Queen, is the extraordinary 100 kg Gold Maple issued by Canada in 2007. It contains 3,215 troy ounces of pure gold, and has a face value

NEWFOUNDLAND
POSTAGE
H.R.H. PRINCESS ELIZABETH
6 SIX CENTS 6

471

Two images have dominated her stamps: the youthful photographic portraits taken by Dorothy Wilding, which set a tone of regal authority, and a second image created by Arnold Machin from a sculpted relief in 1967. Even after 50 years it remains in use, and all attempts to replace it have been strenuously resisted. Machin also devised the portrait head for the first decimal series of Her Majesty's coinage, one of five that have been used in Great Britain through her reign.

479

JAMAICA

£1

TOBACCO GROWING & CIGAR MAKING

474

of a million Canadian dollars. It is worth over £3 million on today's bullion market.

477 The tiniest denomination and one of the most curious examples of The Queen's money was the one cent banknote from Hong Kong. It was first issued in 1941 due to a shortage of coins, and then somehow hung around for another 50 years. Strangely it was taken very seriously for the payment of debt, but the banks saw it as a 'minor administrative irritant'. With a convertible value of more than ten to the British penny, it usually ended up as a souvenir or a bookmark. The micro-note was finally withdrawn in 1995, as the end of British rule in Hong Kong loomed.

478 When The Queen's reign began, the lowest copper in British pockets was the farthing, depicting a little wren. The coin was designed by the Australian artist Harold Wilson Parker for the abandoned coinage of King Edward VIII in 1937, but was kept on and survived until the mid-1950s. Even by then the farthing had become worth almost nothing, and was last minted in 1956. It was demonetised in 1960.

479 Just before Christmas 1937, a 10-year-old Princess Elizabeth was taken by her grandmother Queen Mary to visit the Royal Mint in London. She was given a small selection of souvenir coins from the British Empire to mark her visit.

They were uniface – struck only on one side. Among a little collection of Fiji, Ireland and Mauritius, they included an Australian penny of 1937, depicting a kangaroo. The 1937 Australian penny was never issued and is of the highest rarity. This example, struck in silver, is unique.

480 Such is the power of The Queen's image that many countries issue stamps with her image, despite having no connection to Britain at all. They reflect the fact that there's money to be made issuing purely collectible issues which may never pass through the mail. Among the more strange issuing countries is North Korea, which issued an 80 won sheetlet in 1984.

Ten royal souvenirs

There's nothing like a coronation or a royal wedding to spawn a plethora of royal memorabilia, and The Queen's long reign has provided rich pickings!

481
This retro-style activity book must have provided hours of innocent fun…

482
Temporary tattoos, some of a range of cheeky royal-related designs by graphic artist Lydia Leith.

483
This 'Deluxe Queen Duck' rubber collectible is definitely too grand for bath time!

484
Time for knee – this respectful little mug was produced for the Silver Jubilee in 1977.

485
This is the only time The Queen is likely to be in hot water!

486
We thought we'd join in the fun – this cute corgi Christmas tree decoration comes from Historic Royal Palaces!

487
What better to put atop a Victoria sandwich than these Golden Jubilee cake decorations?

488
Does this souvenir jigsaw from 1948 celebrating Prince Charles's birth qualify as a family heirloom?

489
Knit one pearl one – make your own woolly royal couple.

490
If Her Majesty had tried it, Ma'am might have liked this Diamond Jubilee Special Edition of the famous yeasty spread.

Named in her honour

Over the decades of her reign, The Queen has been commemorated all over the globe. Buildings, islands, bridges, ships and one of the most iconic towers in the world now bear her name.

491 A major new rail line opening in December 2018, stretching more than 60 miles, from Reading to Abbey Wood, via Heathrow Airport, will be named the Elizabeth Line after The Queen. The line, built as part of the Crossrail project, includes 41 fully-accessible stations. The Jubilee Line on the London Underground was named in honour of her Silver Jubilee, but this is the first line to bear The Queen's name.

492 The *Queen Elizabeth 2*, best known as the 'QE2', was a luxury transatlantic liner and cruise ship built by the Cunard company. From 1969 she was Cunard's flagship, until she was retired in 2008. In 2010 Cunard launched its latest luxury ship, the *Queen Elizabeth*.

493 The Queen Elizabeth National Park in Uganda spans over 750 square miles and is home to around 100 species of mammal and over 500 species of birds. Wildlife to be seen in the national park includes leopards, chimpanzees, elephants, hippopotami, crocodiles and lions. The park was founded in 1952 and given its present name in 1954, after The Queen visited Uganda.

494 A cluster of islands off the coast of northern Canada were named the Queen Elizabeth Islands, following her coronation. The islands were formerly known to European settlers as the Parry Islands, after the 19th-century Arctic explorer Sir William Parry.

495 In 1954 horticulturalist Dr Walter Lammerts cultivated a new rose, which he named the Queen

Opposite page:
The Queen looks delighted with her commemorative plaque, given to her by Crossrail workers after she formally unveiled the new round for London's Crossrail 'Elizabeth Line', opening in December 2018.

Below: **The original QE2, built by Cunard in 1969, leaves Sydney Harbour in 2008. (Inset) The lovely Queen Elizabeth rose, first cultivated in 1954.**

Elizabeth. The deep pink rose has won a number of medals and become popular with rose lovers all over the world. In 1979 it was inducted in the Rose Hall of Fame.

496 In 1966 The Queen visited the British Virgin Islands for the first time, where she was invited to open a new bridge, which connected the island of Tortola with Beef Island, the site of the international airport. The bridge was named the Queen Elizabeth II Bridge in her honour (although it's also known as the Beef Island Bridge). In 2002 a new bridge replaced the one opened by The Queen, but retained the regal name.

497 In 2017 The Queen and Prince Philip travelled on a new prototype hybrid train, accompanied by descendants of the great Victorian railway engineer Isambard Kingdom Brunel, who had built the railway on which their train was running. At Paddington Station The Queen unveiled one of the new train's engines, named *Queen Elizabeth II.*

ELIZABETH CELEBRATED

155

The elegant Queen
Elizabeth II Great Court
at the heart of the
British Museum
in London.

(Below) The Queen unveils Great Western Railway's new Intercity Express train at Paddington Station in June 2017; (bottom) Princess Elizabeth Land in the Antarctic was named by explorers from the Discovery Antarctic Expedition; (right) the Elizabeth Tower, Westminster, London, renamed in 2012.

498 The Queen Elizabeth II Great Court at the British Museum in London was opened by The Queen in 2000. The largest covered square in Europe, it was developed from an original Colin St John Wilson design by architects Foster + Partners.

499 Before she even became the monarch, The Queen had an area of the Antarctic named after her. Princess Elizabeth Land was 'discovered' by a joint British, Australian and New Zealand research expedition, led by the explorer Sir Douglas Mawson, who named it after the young princess. The land is claimed by Australia.

500 There are buildings and structures all over the world named after The Queen, including hospitals located as far apart as Welwyn Garden City in Hertfordshire and Kota Kinabalu, Malaysia. In London the structure that houses the world famous Great Bell of the clock nicknamed Big Ben was once known simply as the clock tower, until it was renamed Elizabeth Tower in 2012.

INDEX

PICTURE CREDITS

Abbreviations: b = bottom, c = centre, l = left, r = right, t = top

Alamy: 152cr (Rex Argent/Alamy/Carltonware), 153br (XYZ Pictures/with kind permission of Unilever UK); **ArenaPal:** 148tl (Johan Persson), 148b (Collection Christophel); **Bridgeman Images:** 146tl (Bridgeman Images/Private Collection/Abbott and Holder, London, UK), 150tl (Bridgeman Images/The Royal Mint Museum, UK), 151bc (Bridgeman Images/British Library/© British Library Board. All rights reserved.); **Bud Duck UK Ltd:** 152tr; **Camera Press, London:** 54tl (photograph by Matt Holyoak), 65r (Photograph by Yousef Karsh), 144tc (Photograph by Pietro Annigoni); © Canada Post Corporation, 1932. Reproduced with permission (photograph: Library and Archives Canada): 151tl; © Cartoon Museum Collection: 147bl; **Daily Mail/** cartoon by Mac (Solo Syndication): 146cr; www.donkey-products.com: 152br; **Eyevine/Piero Oliosi/Polaris:** 152cl; **Gerald Scarfe:** 147tl; **Getty Images:** 1 (Matthew Cavanaugh/AFP), 2–3 (Chris Jackson – WPA Pool), 5 (Lisa Sheridan/Studio Lisa/Hulton Archive), 9 (Picture Post/Hulton Archive), 10t (Bob Thomas/Popperfoto), 11tl (Lisa Sheridan/Studio Lisa), 11tr (Universal History Archive), 12tl (Popperfoto), 12–13 (Popperfoto), 13tr (Universal History Archive/UIG), 13br (Popperfoto), 14t (Popperfoto), 14b (Sion Touhig), 15 (Photo12/UIG), 16bl (Popperfoto), 16br (Hulton Archive), 18tl (Hulton Archive), 18tr (Universal History Archive/UIG), 18b (J.A. Hampton/PNA Rota), 19 (PNA Rota), 20tl (Edward G. Malindine/Topical Press Agency), 20tr (Bettmann), 21tl (Rolls Press/Popperfoto), 21tr (John Stillwell – WPA Pool), 21bl (Tim Graham), 24tr (Fox Photos), 24bl (Tim Graham), 25tl (Carl Court/AFP), 26l (Matthew Cavanaugh/AFP), 27tcr (Keystone/Hulton Archive), 27tr (Kieran Doherty/AFP), 27bl (Tim Graham), 28cl (Max Mumby/Indigo), 28tr (Lichfield), 28br (Mark Cuthbert/UK Press), 29tl (Slim Aarons), 29cl (Keystone), 29bl (Tim Graham), 29tr (Indigo), 29br (Bettmann), 30 (Hulton-Deutsch Collection/Corbis Historical), 31br (Lisa Sheridan/Studio Lisa), 32br (Bettmann), 33 (Keystone-France/Gamma-Rapho), 36 (Bentley Archive/Popperfoto), 37tr (Hannah McKay – WPA Pool), 38tl (Photoshot), 38tr (Keystone-France/Gamma-Rapho), 38bc (Buyenlarge), 39 (Anwar Hussein), 40tc (Tim Graham), 40bl (© Hulton-Deutsch Collection/Corbis), 40cr (Central Press/Hulton Archive), 40br (Fox Photos/Hulton Archive), 41t (Lichfield), 41bl (Lichfield), 41bc (Central Press/Hulton Archive), 41br (Lichfield), 44bl (Keystone-France/Gamma-Keystone), 44br (Popperfoto), 45 (Central Press/Hulton Archive), 46cl (Central Press), 46r (J.A. Hampton/Topical Press Agency), 47t (Topical Press Agency), 47br (Picture Post/Hulton Archive), 49tl (Torsten Blackwood/AFP), 49tr (Ron Galella/WireImage), 50 (Jonathan Brady – WPA Pool), 54bl (Fox Photos/Hulton Archive), 55tl (Keystone-France/Gamma-Keystone), 55tr (Fox Photos/Hulton Archive), 55cl (Ian Waldie), 56–7 (Tim Graham), 60l (Hulton-Deutsch Collection/Corbis), 67br (Stephen Hird/WPA Pool), 69r (Shaun Curry/AFP), 82r (Keystone-France/Gamma-Keystone), 83cl (Andrew Winning – WPA Pool), 87 (Keystone-France/Gamma-Rapho), 88bl (Dennis Oulds/Central Press/Hulton Archive), 88–9 (Terry O'Neill/Iconic Images), 89bl (Fox Photos/Hulton Archive), 89tr (Keystone-France/Gamma-Keystone), 91bl (Popperfoto), 91bc (NASA/The LIFE Premium Collection), 92tl (© Hulton-Deutsch Collection/Corbis), 92cl (Colin McPherson/Corbis), 92bl (Owen Humphreys – WPA Pool), 95tr (Rolls Press/Popperfoto), 98–9 (Popperfoto), 100 (Popperfoto), 101t (Popperfoto), 106br (Bettmann), 107 (Kirsty Wigglesworth/AFP), 108–9 (Alastair Grant – WPA Pool), 108bl (Sean Dempsey/AFP), 109bl (ullstein bild), 109cr (Georges De Keerle), 110–11 (Tim Graham), 114t (Topical Press Agency/Hulton Archive), 114–15 (Tim Graham), 115br (Miguel Medina/AFP), 116tr (Keystone-France/Gamma-Keystone), 116bc (Anwar Hussein), 117t (Peter Halmagyi/AFP), 117bl (Chris Ratcliffe/AFP), 117br (Walter Dhladhla/AFP), 118–19 (Martin Godwin), 120tc (Juliette Lasserre/BIPs), 120tr (Monty Fresco), 120b (J.A. Hampton/Topical Press Agency), 121 (Popperfoto), 122bl (Georges De Keerle), 122br (Georges De Keerle), 123b (Leon Neal/AFP), 124tl (Universal History Archive/UIG), 124br (Paul Popper/Popperfoto), 125tc (Catrina Genovese), 125c (Bettmann), 125b (Colin McPherson/Corbis), 128–9 (Suzanne Plunkett/AFP), 130 (Bettmann), 131tl (Michael Ochs Archive), 131bl (Michael Ochs Archive), 131cr (Stephen Wright/Redferns), 132bl (Kevork Djansezian), 132tc (Tim Roney), 133 (Gijsbert Hanekroot/Redferns), 134–5 (The Print Collector), 134b (Metropolitan Police), 135tl (Bettmann), 135tr (Bettmann), 135cl (Bettmann), 135bl (Chris Ware/Keystone/Hulton Archive), 136tl (© Norman Parkinson Archive/Iconic Images), 137tl (Ronald Dumont), 137b (WPA Pool), 138tr (Jean-Claude Deutsch/Paris Match), 139 (Chris Jackson), 147tr (Lexington Herald-Leader/MCT), 149t (Olivier Morin/AFP), 150bcl (Toru Yamanaka/AFP), 154 (Richard Pohle – WPA Pool), 155br (Manuel Litran/Paris Match), 156 (Richard Bryant), 157tl (Chris Jackson), 157bc (© Hulton-Deutsch Collection/Corbis); © Historic Royal Palaces/www.images.hrp.org.uk: 104 (Andrew Butler), 105bc, 153tl; © Ian Jones/ianjonesphoto.co.uk: 74–5, 76tl, 76–7; © Illustrated London News Ltd/Mary Evans: 10br, 62tl, 99, 102tl; Island Records (photo: Charles Moriarty): 132tc; © John Frost Newspapers/Mary Evans Picture Library: 16tc; Lydia Leith Design/www.lydialeith.com: 152bl; Mary Evans Picture Library: 61r; Mary Evans Picture Library/Courtesy of The Land of Lost Content Collection: 153cr; Mary Evans/Grenville Collins Postcard Collection: 10bl; Mary Evans Picture Library/Hardy Amies London: 27bc, 62br; Mary Evans/The Scout Association: 62tr; McLaggan Smith/www.msmugs.com: 147br; New Zealand Post: 150bcr; News Licensing/Andy Davey: 146tr, 146br; © National Portrait Gallery, London: 65cl; National Portrait Gallery/© Chris Levine: 145; National Portrait Gallery, London/© William Hustler and Georgina Hustler: front cover, 23, 65bl, 143tr; PA Images: 25cl, 25bl (Chris Ison/PA Archive), 28bl, 95bl (Chris Jackson/PA Archive), 25r (Chris Radburn/PA Archive), 26tr, 26br, 27tl, 27tcl, 55bl, 59, 60br, 61t, 70bl, 71tl, 71cl, 71cr, 82bl, 83cr, 84–5, 91br, 94, 100b (PA Archive/PA), 27br (Paul Faith/PA Archive), 28tl, 75 (Anwar Hussein/EMPICS Entertainment), 31tc (© EMPICS/PA Archive), 37bl (Neil Munns/PA Archive), 51tl, 70t, 92–3, 96bl (John Stillwell/PA Archive), 51tcl (Martin Rickett/PA Wire), 51bc (Khan Tariq Mikkel/Ritzau), 54tr (Toby Melville/PA Archive), 54br (Fiona Hanson/PA Archive), 55cr (Daniel Leal-Olivas/PA Archive), 55br (Matt Dunham/PA Archive), 67tl (Mike Egerton/PA Archive), 68–9 (Steve Parsons/PA Archive), 72tl (Jeremy Selwyn/PA Archive), 76bl (Lewis Whyld/PA Archive), 90 (S&G/Barratts/EMPICS Sport), 96tl (Ron Bell/PA Archive), 106bl (Keystone Press Agency/Zuma Press), 123t (Howard Jones/CrowdSpark), 128bl (Steve Parsons/PA Archive), 135cr (Topham Picturepoint), 136tr (Lauren Hurley/PA Archive), 138 (Tim Goode/PA Archive), 144tr (Peter Jordan/PA Archive); PUNCH Magazine Cartoon Archive: 146bl; REX/Reginald Davis: 24tl, 24bc, 24br; REX/Shutterstock: 129r; REX/Shutterstock/APA-PictureDesk GmbH: 102–3; REX/Shutterstock/ITV: 146tc; REX/Shutterstock/Ivy Press: 153cl; REX/Shutterstock/James D. Morgan: 155t; REX/Shutterstock/John Melhuish: 105t; REX/Shutterstock/Tim Rooke: 66l, 80–81; REX/Valentin Wolf/imageBROKER: 157r; Ronald Grant Archive: 149br; © Royal Collection Trust/All Rights Reserved: 102br, 142; Royal Collection Trust/© Her Majesty Queen Elizabeth II 2018: 17, 64l, 64tr, 65tl, 72tr, 72bl, 72br, 72–3, 73tr, 73c, 73cr, 73br, 73bl, 151tr; Stamp designs © Royal Mail Group Limited: 150cl, 150cr; By kind permission of the Royal Variety Charity (photograph: HRP/Claire Collins): 83tr; Talking Tables/www.talkingtables.co.uk: 153tr; © 2018 The Andy Warhol Foundation for the Visual Arts, Inc./Licensed by DACS, London, 2018/Photograph: Royal Collection Trust: 141; © The Estate of Feliks Topolski/Photograph: Royal Collection Trust: 143br; TopFoto.co.uk: 144tc, 32tr, 40tl; TopFoto.co.uk/AP: 32lc; Topfoto.co.uk/EMPICS: 48; Topfoto.co.uk/PA Photos: 40tr, 43, 97, 110l, 112–13, 113b, 126–7; Topfoto.co.uk/UPP: 114b; Trunk Archive, NYC/© 2016 Annie Liebovitz: 52–3; Victoria and Albert Museum, London/Cecil Beaton Archive: 63, 67tr, 143cl; © Dean and Chapter of Westminster: 144bl.

This edition © Scala Arts & Heritage Publishers Ltd, 2018
Text © Historic Royal Palaces, 2018

First published in 2018 by
Scala Arts & Heritage Publishers Ltd
10 Lion Yard
Tremadoc Road
London SW4 7NQ, UK
www.scalapublishers.com

In association with
Historic Royal Palaces

Historic Royal Palaces is the charity that looks after:
Tower of London
Hampton Court Palace
Banqueting House
Kensington Palace
Kew Palace
Hillsborough Castle
We help everyone explore the story of how monarchs and people have shaped society, in some of the greatest palaces ever built.
We raise all our own funds and depend on the support of our visitors, members, donors, sponsors and volunteers.

Historic Royal Palaces is a registered charity (no. 1068852).

ISBN (hardback) 978-1-78551-181-3
ISBN (paperback) 978-1-78551-214-8

Project managed by Johanna Stephenson
Designed by Raymonde Watkins
Editor for Historic Royal Palaces: Sarah Kilby
Picture research by Susan Mennell
Printed in Italy

10 9 8 7 6 5 4 3 2 1

Front cover: *Queen Elizabeth II* by Dorothy Wilding, 1952